Linda Skogrand, PhD
Nikki DeFrain, MS
John DeFrain, PhD
Jean E. Jones, PhD

Surviving and Transcending
a Traumatic Childhood
The Dark Thread

Pre-publication
REVIEWS,
COMMENTARIES,
EVALUATIONS . . .

"The authors were able to discover those among us who are examples of how the human spirit can stay strong despite the challenges that life presents. These courageous individuals who were willing to share how they survived and transcended their awful circumstances are an inspiration for how others can seek to do the same. They provide hope for both victims and professionals seeking to help them that the human spirit can conquer and that change can occur. A wonderful life can be achieved around the Dark Thread."

Kevin N. Barlow, MS
Licensed Marriage and Family Therapist;
Clinical Director, Youthtrack, Utah

"A powerful testament to choice and to the ability to thrive despite extreme adversity, if one is willing to believe in a better future and in oneself. This book should be read by anyone whose childhood experiences left deep scars, either emotional or physical, because you are not alone; others have been there. I am particularly grateful for the 'words of wisdom,' wise statements noted by the study participants and summarized in Chapter 9; they are inspirational and moving."

Rochelle L. Dalla, PhD
Associate Professor,
University of Nebraska–Lincoln

The Haworth Press
New York

Surviving and Transcending a Traumatic Childhood
The Dark Thread

Haworth Series in Marriage & Family Studies
Suzanne K. Steinmetz, PhD, MSW
Editor

Surviving and Transcending a Traumatic Childhood: The Dark Thread by Linda Skogrand, Nikki DeFrain, John DeFrain, and Jean E. Jones

Japanese Family and Society: Words from Tongo Takebe, A Meiji Era Sociologist edited by Teruhito Sako and Suzanne K. Steinmetz

Other titles of related interest:

Homelessness in Rural America: Policy and Programs by John Pardeck and Paul Rollinson

Children's Rights: Policy and Practice, Second Edition by John Pardeck

Social Work Practice with Children and Families: A Family Health Approach by Francis Yuen

Surviving and Transcending a Traumatic Childhood
The Dark Thread

Linda Skogrand, PhD
Nikki DeFrain, MS
John DeFrain, PhD
Jean E. Jones, PhD

The Haworth Press
New York

For more information on this book or to order, visit
http://www.haworthpress.com/store/product.asp?sku=5839

or call 1-800-HAWORTH (800-429-6784) in the United States and Canada
or (607) 722-5857 outside the United States and Canada
or contact orders@HaworthPress.com

PUBLISHER'S NOTE
The development, preparation, and publication of this work has been undertaken with great care. However, the Publisher, employees, editors, and agents of The Haworth Press are not responsible for any errors contained herein or for consequences that may ensue from use of materials or information contained in this work. The Haworth Press is committed to the dissemination of ideas and information according to the highest standards of intellectual freedom and the free exchange of ideas. Statements made and opinions expressed in this publication do not necessarily reflect the views of the Publisher, Directors, management, or staff of The Haworth Press, Inc., or an endorsement by them.

Identities and circumstances of individuals discussed in this book have been changed to protect confidentiality.

Some information in Chapters 2 and 3 was previously published in *Marriage and Family Review*, 35(1/2): 117-146; 37(3): 5-26, published by The Haworth Press, Inc.

Photo image by Dorothy Gay Vela.

Cover design by Marylouise E. Doyle.

Libray of Congress Cataloging-in-Publication Data

Surviving and transcending a traumatic childhood : the dark thread / Linda Skogrand . . . [et al.].
    p. ; cm.
    Includes bibliographical references and index.
    ISBN: 978-0-7890-3264-5 (hard : alk. paper)
    ISBN: 978-0-7890-3265-2 (soft : alk. paper)
    1. Psychic trauma in children. I. Skogrand, Linda.

[DNLM: 1. Stress Disorders, Traumatic. 2. Adaptation, Psychological. 3. Adult. 4. Child. 5. Survivors—psychology. WM 172 S963 2007]

RJ506.P66S87 2007
618.92'8521—dc22

                                           2006031657

ABOUT THE TITLE

The subtitle of this book, The Dark Thread, *was inspired by Joseph Larson, one of the participants in this study, who described how he survived and transcended a traumatic childhood. He compared the traumatic childhood he experienced as a "dark thread woven through a piece of cloth—you can't pull it out without unraveling the whole thing. And it shows up here and there among all the other threads." He has also reviewed the manuscript and provided his thoughts about the book.*

This book is about the experiences of 90 people who believed they had survived and transcended a traumatic childhood. Some of these people experienced severe physical abuse. Others suffered emotional and psychological abuse from parents or other adults in their lives. Many of these individuals probably did not know that what they were suffering as children was traumatic—they may even hesitate to identify it as such today.

When you are a child, it is hard to know what is normal or healthy. One's experiences in a family situation are the only reality there is. On some level, you feel that what is happening is bad or horrible and you wish it would stop. But your parent or sibling may have warned you not to talk to anyone else about these "family problems." As a child, you probably feel that what is happening is somehow your fault and that you deserve this punishment being inflicted on you.

It takes years to transcend a traumatic childhood. It is not something that you ever really "get over." On some level, the experience stays with you throughout your life. As the title of this book suggests, you never really escape the past—for better or worse, it is always part of who you are.

It is like a dark thread that is woven into a beautifully colored cloth; you cannot pull out that thread without unraveling the whole thing. It shows up here and there among all the other threads. You cannot remove it—and perhaps would never choose to do so—because it would change the tapestry that is you.

If you experienced physical or emotional abuse or neglect as a child, I hope that you will find affirmation and inspiration in these stories. Just hearing that someone else has walked a similar path can be affirming of your own life journey. The journey to health is long and really never ends. The death of a loved one, the loss of a job, the diagnosis of a severe illness, or other difficult life experiences can bring back those old feelings of helplessness and despair.

Who really knows why some people never recover from childhood abuse—living a lifetime of debilitating fear or depression—and others find ways to survive and transcend this early experience? Some of us have found support in teachers and friends. Some of us just endured the pain and made decisions to move on. Some of us have had years of therapy. Some of us have been lucky enough to find life partners or children who fill our lives with love and meaning.

Transcending a traumatic childhood is about the continuous process of healing. The word *transcend* comes from two Latin words meaning "to climb over." *Transcendence* is defined as "going beyond the ordinary limits." People who have transcended childhood abuse have found ways to climb over huge emotional boulders to live in a way that others would not ordinarily expect after such a childhood.

If you are one of these people, I hope this book reminds you of how far you have come. Yes, there will be more difficult life experiences to deal with at some point in your future. But, like others who have survived and transcended early traumas, you can find comfort in knowing that you have the resources to draw on deep within you to help you deal with whatever your life may bring.

Someday, we will know more about what helps certain individuals survive childhood abuse and its emotional baggage. This book offers new insights to help others transcend this type of experience.

Joseph A. Larson, LISW, MDiv
Executive Director, The Aliveness Project
Minneapolis, Minnesota

ABOUT THE AUTHORS

Linda Skogrand, PhD, is an assistant professor and extension specialist at Utah State University in Logan. Her early career was as a social worker where she provided services and education to low income families in inner-city communities. In addition to research about traumatic childhoods, she has done research in the following areas: families who have experienced Sudden Infant Death (SIDS); values in parent education; and equity and equality in vocational education. Her current research interests focus on what makes strong marriages in diverse cultures. She has served as director of the Community/University Partnership in Education and Service (CUPES), a Kellogg funded project that developed a partnership between the health sciences at the University of Minnesota and an inner-city community in Minneapolis.

Nikki DeFrain, MS, is a homemaker whose master's degree is in family studies with an emphasis on gerontology. With her husband John DeFrain, she has traveled around the world learning about families in many cultures. She has worked and volunteered in many positions as a teacher of young children, family studies researcher, conference organizer, counselor of older people and their families, and in various community services.

John DeFrain, PhD, is Professor and Extension Family and Community Development Specialist at the University of Nebraska–Lincoln. For thirty years, he has focused professional interests on research and educational programs to develop couple and family strengths. He has published more than ninety professional articles and co-authored and co-edited eighteen books on family issues, including *Marriage and Family: Diversity and Strengths, 5th Edition;* and *Building Relationships: Developing Skills for Life.*

Jean E. Jones, PhD, is Marketing Director for Concordia University on Seward, Nebraska, and serves on the faculty as an adjunct professor in the areas of research design and psychology. Formerly the director of a federal technology grant, Dr. Jones also served as president of her local school board and as a member of the Nebraska Council of Teacher Education. She has co-authored several articles in the area of technology integration evaluation and family strengths.

CONTENTS

Foreword

Surviving and Transcending a Traumatic Childhood: The Dark Thread weaves together a series of stories that creates a silver lining. Rather than traumatic events leading to dysfunction, these are stories of hope where individuals not just survive, but thrive. The people telling their stories transcended their circumstances and became healthier because of their struggles.

While many books have been written about abuse and its negative consequences, this book not only documents the struggles and endless challenges of many children and adults, but also their many triumphs. The field needs more positive and affirming success stories like this, demonstrating the importance of building on strengths.

Sorting through over 2,500 pages of in-depth and revealing personal stories from ninety people was not an easy task for the four authors. Each of the ninety participants wrote twenty-five to fifty page answers to questions about their struggles. While the authors found it emotionally draining just to read the stories, their task was more hopeful as they distilled the underlying themes and identified the coping resources that were used by this diverse group of people.

The resources that helped these individuals thrive were their amazing capacity for growth, their dissociation from the situation, and their ability to escape emotionally from the traumatic events. Being proactive and using spiritual resources also helped them demonstrate amazing resiliency.

"Significant other" adults were also critical in helping these individuals transcend their circumstances. By getting away from the family, which was often the source of abuse, the participants were provided a refuge and a support system by way of people who came into their lives.

Surviving and Transcending a Traumatic Childhood
© 2007 by The Haworth Press, Inc. All rights reserved.
doi:10.1300/5839_a

These stories are poignant and emotionally gripping. This book brings hope and a positive spirit to lives that were filled with so much suffering. Truly, these stories are dark threads that have created a silver lining for us to learn from and we can rejoice in the stories of achievement and resiliency.

David H. Olson, PhD
Professor Emeritus
Family Social Science
University of Minnesota

Acknowledgments

We began gathering data for this book several years ago and knew there was great wisdom in the testimony of those who participated in the study. We hoped there would be a time when the stories would be told to those who could benefit from the experiences of those who survived and transcended. As authors, we have overwhelming gratitude for those who participated in the research study and ultimately allowed their stories to be shared with others. Many of the participants said it was difficult and painful, and yet, many said they did it because it might help someone else on the journey toward healing.

If this book is of value to you as a reader, know that the book exists only because others had the courage to tell their story—some for the very first time—and describe what helped them in their process of healing. We, as researchers, have said many times, "We are only the vehicle for making their stories accessible to others."

We thank Gary Peterson and Suzanne Steinmetz, editors of the research journal *Marriage and Family Review.* They are editors of the journal that published articles from the data and supported the writing of this book. We thank The Haworth Press for publishing our book and getting the information into the hands of the people who can benefit from the experiences of those who have come through the healing process. Although we as researchers have a goal of publishing in professional journals, we all also have a desire to get the information we gather into the hands of the lay public. That is where the information about surviving and transcending traumatic childhoods came from, and that is where it needs to end up. If lay people cannot benefit from our work, then there is no reason to do what we do.

We have talked about the findings from this study at conferences, public presentations, in the Cooperative Extension arena, in classes, with friends and relatives, and with anyone else who would listen.

Surviving and Transcending a Traumatic Childhood
© 2007 by The Haworth Press, Inc. All rights reserved.
doi:10.1300/5839_b

When we talked about this research, we were told over and over again that these stories needed to be told. We thank all of you who have encouraged us in our efforts to see this product through to publication.

We as researchers have all come from families that have supported us in our work, including the writing of this book. We would like to thank Steven, Sara, Jennifer, Aaron, Amie, Alyssa, Erica, Dave, John, and Anne. Finally, we would like to thank Steven Gilbertson who edited several versions of the manuscript.

Chapter 1

Introduction

I believe that man will not merely endure: he will prevail. He is immortal, not because he alone among creatures has an inexhaustible voice, but because he has a soul, a spirit capable of compassion and sacrifice and endurance . . . the writer's duty is to write about these things. It is his privilege to help man endure by lifting his heart, by reminding him of the courage and honor and hope and pride and compassion and pity and sacrifice which have been the glory of his past . . . [the writer's] voice need not merely be the record of man, it can be one of the props, the pillars to help him endure and prevail.

William Faulkner

This introductory quote, taken from William Faulkner's (1965) acceptance speech upon receiving the Nobel Prize for Literature in 1950, describes what this book is about: how the *souls* of people who have had traumatic things happen to them as children are able to rise above all this and not only *endure* the trauma, but are able to *prevail*. Although we will use different terms to describe this phenomenon, essentially we are talking about the same concepts as Faulkner. We are talking about the ability of the human spirit not only to *survive* but to *transcend* the horrible things that happen. What goes through the minds of people as they are experiencing the trauma? What are the life-saving survival strategies people use to not only get through it, but then rise above it all? What is this process of surviving and transcending all about?

Surviving and Transcending a Traumatic Childhood
© 2007 by The Haworth Press, Inc. All rights reserved.
doi:10.1300/5839_01

The experts in this book are not the authors, but rather the people who had the courage to spend painful hours telling the stories of what happened to them as children: who or what they hung on to for hope, how they got through it, and, more importantly, the process they went through to become healthy, happy adults. As we read the stories of those who survived and transcended traumatic childhoods, we would shake our heads and exclaim, "How did they do it?" Individuals would often identify people or personal qualities or abilities which helped them, such as a belief in God, a loving sister, a teacher, being smart, being a good basketball player, or having the courage not to act like those who had hurt them. But, we would ask ourselves, what gave them the strength and hope that things would ever change and the ability to hang on until those changes came? The recurring answer can only be the human spirit.

Many of the people whose lives are described in this book had nothing left as children except their own indomitable spirit. Our understanding of the ability of the human spirit to prevail which came from these stories is best summarized by Muriel and John James (1992) in their book, *Passions for Life: Psychology and the Human Spirit*. They define it this way: "The human spirit is the vital animating force that can move a person beyond the normal confines of life to a sense of wholeness and holiness" (p. 20). These authors go on to say the human spirit is sometimes called the *soul,* and even though it is not tangible, it can be experienced, understood, and expressed. These authors also say that when individuals are constrained, intimidated, or abused, as the people in this book have been, they will *struggle* for their spirit to be free. This cry will come from the depths of the human spirit. We encourage you to watch for evidence of the workings of the human spirit as you read this book.

IMPORTANCE OF THE TOPIC

What are the long-term effects of childhood trauma and abuse? The findings are mixed. Research indicates that trauma or abuse has touched the lives of a significant number of children. It is estimated that one out of four adults has suffered from child abuse (Valentine & Feinaurer, 1993). In addition to the actual abuse which has been studied, children have and will continue to face other stresses in their environment such as neglect, war, poverty, and alienation from their parents, to name a few. Though 40 percent of survivors showed poor recovery from abuse, others showed significant recovery (Browne & Finkelhor, 1986). Childhood abuse has been found to have detrimental effects on the overall well-being of the survivors (Kennedy & Drebing, 2002). Individuals who suffer from abuse are more likely to show emotional, psychosocial, and behavioral problems than those who have not been abused.

Researchers have also learned that childhood abuse or trauma affect one's ability to function in relationships and family life. For example, Wampler and Nelson (2000) looked at the association between traumatic childhood events such as physical abuse, sexual abuse, or loss through death, and subsequent relationship satisfaction in couples seeking clinical help. They concluded that there is a possible indirect effect of childhood loss and trauma on current relationship functioning. Oz (2001) found in a study of women that, during the therapeutic process, the abused survivor confronted her pain and fear, and this effort drew energy previously used in day-to-day functioning at work and at home. In the more severe cases, dealing with the pain was so difficult it allowed only for getting through the day. This drain of energy also had an effect on the surivivor's spouse's sense of well-being in the marriage relationship and on the marital system as well.

With such a high rate of people who have experienced abuse or other childhood trauma, and the fact that, for most, it affects their adult relationships and family life, it is critical to identify ways to support these adults through the healing process. It is also important to find out what works, from the perspective of the experts—those who have had the experience.

ABOUT THE STUDY

We are using several terms in this book that should be described and discussed. Two of these terms are *survived* and *transcended.* A dictionary definition of surviving would say something about the ability to "continue to exist" or say simply "to stay alive." An individual who survives a traumatic childhood exists, and may even function in society, but the trauma still continues to control the person's life. It negatively affects self-esteem. It keeps people from doing things they would like to do because of the scripts and messages that are still alive as a result of the trauma. We have included survivors in this book as well as those who have transcended to illustrate that this progression from surviving to transcending is a continuum. Even those who feel they have transcended would say that the journey is never done. New issues or life changes come up which must be addressed as they relate to the traumatic childhood.

A person who has transcended the trauma is basically a healthy adult who somehow (and that is what this book is about) has risen above what happened in his or her childhood. A transcendent person is an emotionally balanced person who is happy with herself or himself and whose past does not control the future. Our request for participants, published in newspapers around the country, described *transcended* as "those who feel they are now relatively happy, well-adjusted individuals." Transcendent individuals are those who are as healthy today as before the trauma occurred and might even say things like, "This experience has made me a better person. I now understand pain which helps me help others." One woman said that all of her horrible childhood experiences helped her grow and come closer to her adult goal of breaking a generational chain of dysfunction. The stories included in this book also include people who were born into families where chaos prevailed. They could not return to a state of health before the trauma because trauma is all they knew. How did these people know they could attain something they had never experienced? These individuals would say things like, "I just knew there was something better. I knew I could rise above this. I could not stand this ugly life." These stories truly are examples of the triumph of the human spirit.

People may also wonder what we mean by *traumatic*. A traumatic event is an event which has a lasting emotional or psychological effect on one's life. A traumatic childhood can be described as one that is not focused on one event, but rather prolonged abuse, neglect, or other severe stressors. Our newspaper story described trauma as "severe and/or prolonged psychological stress." Each individual who read the news story determined for herself or himself whether their childhood had been traumatic. We are aware that different individuals may perceive the same event differently.

A twenty-three-page open-ended questionnaire was developed, based on the existing research literature in this area of study and on the four authors' many years of learning about families in crisis. The research questions in the instrument have roots in several conceptual frameworks or theories:

- family stress and crisis theories
- biopsychosocial stress theories
- family systems frameworks
- family ecological frameworks
- life-span development theories
- family strengths perspective
- resilient children theories
- family therapy models
- family education models
- individual psychotherapy models
- qualitative research literature

We wanted to look at *how* people survived and transcended a tragically difficult childhood. We analyzed written testimony from people who have survived and transcended, in their judgment. We believe that the study of their lives yields important insights into the processes by which people grow to be healthy adults and that these insights can be useful to those who are working with family members seeking to transcend the difficulties of their past.

The goal of our many questions was to help individuals tell their stories. We explained in the covering letter to the questionnaire that we wanted participants to answer the open-ended questions in their own way, to take as much space as they needed, and not to worry about spelling, punctuation, and grammar. We wanted them to know that their testimony could help others deal with similar difficulties.

Individuals were asked to participate in the study through newspaper solicitation. Approximately 500 letters were sent to newspapers throughout the United States. These newspapers and addresses were obtained from the *Gale Directory of Publications and Broadcast Media*. We sent letters to a mix of large newspapers and small newspapers; urban, suburban, and rural newspapers; community newspapers; and to self-help newspapers. We asked the newspapers to publish our request for participants in their family life or special features section at their convenience. We have no idea which newspapers published our story. However, the letters from people who wanted to participate in the study began to come in from all over the United States. In the end, we had 252 requests for questionnaires from twenty-four states, from Alaska to Texas and from Washington State to Georgia. The requests came from rural, urban, and suburban areas.

Questionnaires were sent to the people who responded to our story in the newspapers, along with a self-addressed stamped envelope. A covering letter was attached to the questionnaire explaining that their responses would be anonymous and that we did not want the participants to include their name or address on the questionnaire. We encouraged participants to talk with a trusted friend or professional if the instrument created anguish for them. We let them know that if some questions were too painful, they should skip them. If the process of completing the instrument became too painful, they were encouraged to "throw it away."

We wanted people to realize that this process would probably be painful, but their stories would be helpful to others who had experienced trauma and the professionals who help them. The participants, however, needed to be the judge as to whether they wanted to participate in the study. We explained that the findings would be published in a book written for survivors, those who had transcended, and those who might be in a position to help those who were in the process of surviving and transcending. We were deliberate in not giving people a deadline for returning the questionnaires. We did not want to push. We received the last questionnaire two years after it was mailed out.

At the end of the questionnaire we included several paragraphs thanking participants for participating and suggesting that they might want to make a copy of their responses to keep as a milepost in the months and years to come. We, again, encouraged participants to talk with a trusted relative, friend, or professional if they felt distress in the process of completing the questionnaire. We ended by saying we hoped this process was a positive experience in their process of transcending.

The letters we received asking for the questionnaire were interesting in and of themselves. Some simply sent postcards requesting the instrument with their name and address. Others sent one-page letters briefly explaining the trauma, then described what they are now doing to in some way show us they are healthy adults. Some included business cards or brochures describing their profession, which often was work in a helping profession. Several people included even a résumé describing their achievements to prove they had transcended. Others sent very long letters describing in detail many aspects of the trauma and their recovery. Many said they wanted to participate, "if it could help someone else."

Some people had personal motives for wanting to participate in the study. One person said, "One of the missing pieces for me has been an opportunity to tell my story to someone who really wants to hear it." Another person said, "I am currently going through counseling to help deal with several issues in my life. . . . I feel that it might help me face up to my past and come to terms with things if I participate in your study."

There were many people who commended us for our approach to the study. One person said, "It's about time someone is addressing this issue (transcending) instead of just blaming their childhood for failures." Another person said, "We hear so many of the horror stories of folks like myself who have suffered tremendously painful childhoods, but we don't hear the good news that there is hope for recovery and, yes, even joy!" Another person explained that society has spent so much time talking about people who do not survive and not enough on the ones who live happy and have productive lives.

Although most people who wrote were supportive of our study, one person was skeptical. The letter began with several questions, "Happy compared to what?" "What's the difference between transcending and transcended?" "How do I know you're not just another voyeur?" "What do you know about conservative German Lutheran psychosis?" "What will *you* get out of this?" And, "What's in it for me, especially if you publish an eyebrow-raising bestseller?" Another person said, "I hope this isn't some bogus article because you will be playing with peoples' emotions."

The questionnaires began to come in, slowly and steadily. Some people limited their answers to the space on the twenty-three-page instrument. Others included handwritten or typed pages to elaborate on their answers. Some included copies of their life story which had been written for college courses or therapy. Many included poetry or stories they had written during their process of transcending and many of these poems and stories are included in this book.

One person kept the questionnaire for five months before beginning to work on it and then was only able to complete two pages. This person wrote, "I'm sorry I can't finish this. I've already made in-depth reports such as you request to myself and in my journal, and I can't bear to do that again. I hope your book will help others."

The time, energy, and pain to complete the questionnaire was considerable. One person said it took fifteen hours. Another said it took five hours to complete, but had to be done over four days. One person said she began the questionnaire, came to an issue she had not resolved, went back into therapy, and then finished the questionnaire. Several people completed the questionnaire by saying they shed tears while writing it. Many thanked us for doing the study and said it helped in their process of transcending to participate in the study. One person wrote on the bottom of the last page of the questionnaire, "It's all true!" as if we would not believe it.

One person began his story by saying, "Oh shit, I really don't want to do this. Hell! Oh, all right, here goes. I'm going to stick to the main themes because it would take a lot of paper to go into detail." The longest response we received was from a person who added forty-four single-spaced typed pages to the questionnaire. In all we received 102 questionnaires (40.4 percent of the total of 252 requests). Ninety of the questionnaires (35.7 percent) were satisfactorily completed and legible.

ABOUT THE PARTICIPANTS

So, what were the traumatic childhood experiences described by our participants? Certainly we anticipated experiences with sexual and physical abuse, alcoholism, neglect, and violence. We received many completed questionnaires which described those experiences. However, we also heard stories of many other kinds of traumatic experiences or variations on the above themes which were surprises for us. They were surprises because of the variety of traumatic experiences, the intensity of the stress, and the fact that many people dealt with multiple issues in their childhood. For example, it was not uncommon for one individual to experience alcoholism, physical and sexual abuse, as well as abandonment.

From the very beginning of our work in the area of traumatic childhood, we assumed that abuse would be a very common form of trauma that individuals would report. We did not simply wish to explore abuse alone in this research; instead, we chose to look more broadly at the various traumas people experienced. As we read the responses to the questionnaires, we realized that most of the childhood trauma that participants described was what we typically think of as abuse. This led us to ask, Does trauma equal abuse? We went back and studied the testimony of all ninety respondents who returned complete and legible questionnaires. In eighty-nine out of ninety cases, at least one of the traumatic events they reported to us was a type of abuse. And in further analysis, rereading the participants' written testimonies carefully, we verified that only one person, as far as we can tell from this individual's written report, out of ninety did not experience any form of abuse as a child. Instead of abuse, this person experienced a natural disaster that she believed had long-term, traumatic consequences for her life: a devastating forest fire swept through her community when she was a child. The fire destroyed the family's home and all their possessions, and two of her favorite schoolteachers were burned to death. For the other participants—for 98.8 percent of the people in the study—events in their traumatic childhood included abuse from other people. Most often this abuse was from within the family, but sometimes it was abuse that the members of society inflicted upon an individual or the family. Therefore throughout this book, we will use abuse and trauma interchangeably.

It is, of course, quite possible that some of these stories are not true. We were directed by the institutional review board at our educational institutions to go to great lengths to preserve the anonymity of the participants, and since the participants in the study are anonymous, we have no way of verifying what happened to them. At best, the stories do not necessarily reflect *the truth,* but only the writer's *perception of the truth.* This is an important distinction we need to make here. With these limitations clearly in mind, we still believe that taken as a whole, these stories ring true; they give us a very realistic picture of what traumatic childhood is all about, and how people over the long-term manage to rise above the tragedy of their past.

Toward the end of the questionnaire we asked, "All things considered, have you survived, or have you survived *and* transcended a traumatic childhood?" Remember: our initial newspaper story was asking for volunteers who had both survived and transcended. The vast majority of individuals, after rethinking their lives and filling out the questionnaire, said they had transcended (83.5 percent); but some drew the conclusion on their own that they had only survived, but not transcended (11 percent); and some, for whatever reasons, did not respond to the question (5.5 percent).

Who are the people who participated in the study? Their average age was forty-five years, and ranged from twenty years to people in their seventies. They were primarily European American (88 percent), but there were also individuals that were American Indian (5 percent); African American (3 percent); Latino (1 percent); Asian American (1 percent); and 2 percent who identified themselves as "other."

Of the people who participated in the study, 80 percent were women and 20 percent were men. We often asked ourselves why women were so much more likely than men to volunteer to participate in a study like this. One might speculate that girls are more likely to be abused than boys, and, therefore, there is a greater pool of potential participants for our study who are women. Girls are sexually abused more often than boys (Darkness to Light, 2006). Thus, it is not clear if the potential participant pool for our study had more women in it or more men.

Another possibility would be that women are more likely to be innately and culturally inclined to be in touch with and share their feelings when it comes to a painful subject such as childhood trauma. We have no way of assessing this.

It is also possible that women are more likely to actually transcend childhood trauma than men. Clinicians influenced by family systems theory attribute a tendency toward domestic violence as an adult to growing up in a violent home, where the child learns to be a victim as well as a potential victimizer. Abused male children typically learn to be victimizers. They often develop a sort of "pecking order" attitude toward violence: You get beaten up when you are small, and then when you are big you repeat what you learned as a child. Female children typically learn to be victims in their families of origin and are likely to become victims again in their marriages (Gelles, 2000). Women in our society are socialized to be kind and loving, and men are socialized to be aggressive. Though she may grow up in a violent home, society gives girls and women countless models and social directives indicating that nonviolence is the correct path for a woman. The social directives for men are less clear. Male aggression and dominant behavior are common images in their daily lives. Perhaps it is simply easier or more natural for a man to grow up to become a victimizer, rather than to heal, transcend childhood trauma, and grow into a loving and caring individual. Again, 80 percent of the participants in our study were women, and 20 percent were men. We can only speculate as to why.

INTENDED AUDIENCE

This book is written for all those who have experienced traumatic childhoods and are in the process of surviving and transcending. The people who have told their stories used a variety of resources or life-saving techniques to get through it all. Some of these resources came from within themselves and some came from outside of themselves. These resources are likely to be of help to others who are not as far along in their journey. These resources are uniquely fashioned for each individual, so a person may need to read several stories to find resources that have personal meaning.

Another goal of this book is to give hope to those who feel life is hopeless. Things can get better. Some of the stories in this book are as devastating and painful as life has to offer, and, yet, most of these people were at a point where they had hope for their lives and looked forward to the future.

This book is also written for friends, family, and people in the helping professions who offer support, encouragement, and a listening ear to those who have had painful childhoods. These stories provide a deeper understanding of what is in the hearts and the souls of people who have lived through painful childhoods. It tells untold stories. It speaks truth to a world which most often wants to look the other way. It is written for counselors and therapists who have helped people deal with the pain as it was expressed in counseling sessions, but have not heard how people are doing now, several years down the road. Often, the professional is visited during a time of acute crisis in the life of the individual or the family. The snapshot of crisis the professional sees over six or ten or thirty brief sessions can give her or him a skewed picture of a long, long process. These stories, on the other hand, help put the process in perspective. We get to see *the rest of the story,* and the rest of the story is often quite uplifting. Counselors and therapists need to know this, in order to see how crucial a role they play in many lives.

Finally, this book is written as a testimony for all of us, who at times need to be reminded that the human spirit is indeed strong and can help all of us through seemingly insurmountable pain and difficulty. In Ernest Hemingway's words in *A Farewell to Arms,* "The world breaks everyone and afterward many become strong at the broken places" (1929, p. 229).

ORGANIZATION OF THE BOOK

The next chapter of this book, Chapter 2, is about what happened to the ninety participants in this study as they were children living through the trauma and abuse. It also describes what they did as children to survive. This chapter identifies the major themes that emerged as we looked at the stories of all the participants. Chapter 3 provides a summary of the themes that emerged as we considered the actions taken by all the participants as adults when they began the process of healing and, later, became healthy adults.

Chapters 4 through 8 provide individual stories about the lives of sixteen participants in the study. Each story tells about the trauma these individuals experienced as children, how they survived, and what they did as adults to transcend. They have been divided into five chapters to highlight different patterns that became evident to us as researchers as we read the stories.

Chapter 4 is about four participants who had differing childhood experiences with school life. Did their school situation help or hinder them in their growing up years? The answer to that question varied by participant. Chapter 5 describes the lives of three participants who talk about the role of religion and spirituality in surviving and transcending a traumatic childhood. Chapter 6 is titled "Pariah or Paragon." This chapter highlights the fact that children who were abused came from all kinds of homes. From the outside, some families were viewed as outcasts, or pariahs of society—and abuse occurred. Some families were examples of what appeared to be a perfect family, or paragons of society—and abuse occurred. No one helped the children in either type of family. Chapter 7 highlights the stories of participants in the study who had significant people who helped them along the way. These significant people probably had no idea how important they were in the lives of those who had been abused. Chapter 8 highlights how the childhood trauma, and surviving and transcending that trauma, had positive effects on the participants.

Because the participants typically wrote thirty pages or more as they answered our questions, we have told the participants' stories in Chapters 4 through 8 by focusing on the major events and thoughts about their life experiences. We took sections of the participants' responses from throughout the questionnaire in an effort to put the story in the sequence of how it happened, and then described "how they are today" at the end. We sometimes changed spelling, grammar, and sentence structure for clarity but did not change meaning. We tried as much as possible to keep their words, their phrases, and their emphases intact. Sometimes the grammar was not perfect, but to change it would change the meaning or spirit of the sentence, so we left it as it was. We included their short, clipped sentences because it helped describe the sense of immediacy, urgency, and danger that many stories evoked. Sometimes they would underline a word three times, and we italicized the word to convey this emphasis. They would often begin a sentence with "and" or "but," as if in a conversation with the reader. We left those sentences as they were. Sometimes they swore. We included these angry words. How the story was told *is* part of the story; we do not want to take that away from the telling of it. As we read the stories, we can feel the fear. Our hearts begin to pound. Hell is about to break loose again. As we read the stories, it is as if the reader and the writer are there together in the long ago. The past and the present have become one.

We have changed the identifying names of the people referenced in these stories in order that they remain anonymous. They sometimes talked about their home towns, or where they moved. Again, we changed the names of the places they described to maintain their anonymity.

Finally, Chapter 9 summarizes what we learned from this study and what we might do to help children survive and adults transcend a traumatic childhood. The appendixes include a list of resources that might be helpful to those in the process of transcending and a self study guide for those who want to use questions from the questionnaire as a way to develop a deeper understanding of their own healing process.

Chapter 2

Surviving As Children

We concluded, after reading and studying the stories of people who participated in our study, that children *survived* and adults *transcended* traumatic childhoods. Children had the skills only to get through and, in some cases, do what they had to do to stay alive. Here is a story that one woman told us, which described her response to the abuse in her childhood:

> A little dark-eyed girl sat in a big overstuffed chair. She dared not move or whimper but prayed that her mother would forget she was angry at her. She thought hard, "What did I do now?"
>
> "I'm sorry, I'm sorry, I'm sorry," kept playing over and over in her ears, but she couldn't remember what for. "I did my homework," she reminded herself. "I made my bed this morning and I didn't forget to clean my room."
>
> "I wish I could melt into that wall or change places with my brother. I didn't spill my milk at dinner and tried to clean up the dishes quickly."
>
> She heard her mother's footsteps heavy on the wooden floor above. She heard her scream and knew she would be down soon. She went numb and gritted her teeth, praying for her father to come back, and then lost herself in the cracks in the ceiling. With the first blows to her head . . . "I'm sorry! I'm sorry!"

She only did what a child could do and that was to respond to what came her way. She had no power to do anything else.

Surviving and Transcending a Traumatic Childhood
© 2007 by The Haworth Press, Inc. All rights reserved.
doi:10.1300/5839_02

Sometimes, as children, they could not realize that what was happening to them was abnormal. Twenty percent of the participants indicated that, as children, they thought every child went through what they were going through. If they did realize it was abnormal, how could they do anything but get through it? They typically did not have the cognitive and social skills to know what to do or ask for help. They certainly did not have the physical strength to stave off an attacker. Therefore, as children, they could not heal and become healthy. They could only survive as best they could by responding to each incident as it occurred.

The participants in our study were asked to identify the type or types of trauma they believed they endured as children from a checklist containing twenty-one types of events. Their responses are summarized in Table 2.1. Nearly half of the respondents reported experiencing six to ten forms of trauma during their childhood, and almost a third reported two to five forms. No one experienced only one type of trauma as they were growing up; one person checked all twenty-two items on the list. As stated in the first chapter of this book, eighty-nine of the ninety participants in the study experienced some type of abuse, even though they were responding to a study about traumatic childhoods. Therefore, trauma meant abuse, and the abuse was typically from members of their own family.

BEGINNING OF THE TRAUMA

Almost 30 percent of the individuals in the study did not respond when asked about when the traumatic events in their childhood began; for many, the trauma was always there as a youngster. They were born into a life of difficulties. Similarly, many participants could not pinpoint when the traumatic times ended. In some cases, they were not sure it was really over, even though they were participating in the study as adults believing that they had survived and transcended it. In other cases, the healing was so gradual it was hard to say when the process ended or if it ever would. For the 70 percent who did answer these quantitative-type questions about time frame, the average individual believed the traumatic times began at 4.9 years of age and ended at age 24.0 years. That constituted more than 19 years of difficulty to endure.

TABLE 2.1 Frequency of Types of Traumatic Life Events Experienced by Respondents

Type	%	Frequency
Emotional abuse	87.7	79
Physical abuse	64.4	58
Violence	63.3	57
Sexual abuse	52.2	47
Alcohol or other drug abuse in the family	51.1	46
Abandonment	48.8	44
Alienation	47.7	43
Neglect	47.7	43
Mental illness of a family member	36.6	33
Poverty	34.4	31
Death	34.4	31
Physical illness of a family member	27.7	25
Other[a]	27.7	25
Discrimination	26.6	24
Physical injury	23.3	21
Pregnancy	13.3	12
War	12.2	11
Suicide	11.1	10
Developmental disability	10.0	9
Gay, lesbian, bisexual issues	8.8	8
Homelessness	7.7	7
Natural disaster	5.5	5

[a]Other included abortions, miscarriages, shock treatments, low self-esteem, imprisonment, lack of love, satanic ritual/abuse, parents' divorce, moving constantly, and parents' fights.

How many years had it been since the difficult times in childhood ended? The average was 23.9 years, but frankly, the accounts of childhood trauma were written with such emotional immediacy that the individuals sometimes said it felt as if it had happened only yesterday.

Sometimes the stories were so terrible that we felt incredulous. As researchers, trained to be skeptical and questioning, we found ourselves asking, "Is this true? Did this really happen? Are these so-called false memories?"

And then we would respond to ourselves, "Did the Holocaust happen?"

And we would reply, "Yes, we believe it did."

"And, then, is it possible that these stories are true, also?"

And we would answer, "Yes, it is very possible."

COMMON FEELINGS ASSOCIATED WITH TRAUMA

The pain associated with the individuals' memories of childhood was sometimes staggering for them to recall. We chose to group these feelings into six categories: (1) loneliness and isolation; (2) fear and confusion; (3) bitterness, anger, and sorrow; (4) skepticism and distrust; (5) feeling like I might go crazy; and (6) guilt and blame.

Loneliness and Isolation

Many of the participants described families which were extremely isolated from other people and from each other. A woman who was a sixty-two-year-old retired teacher said, "I never had a childhood. We never went any place with our parents, *not once*. I can never remember having a meaningful conversation with either parent. We never had company. Nobody ever invited our family to their home. Not even relatives." These feelings often led to a sense of desperation:

> I have had thoughts of committing suicide because of the loneliness—so lonely! I think a lot of it is self-esteem.

> * * *

> I felt very lonely and abandoned because we really never physically touched or talked to each other. Nobody, I felt, took care of me as a child. I tried to be a good little girl, but it was out of my control. I educated myself through college, initiated getting my mother to a treatment facility after all six of us children were moved from the parental home. Why didn't someone do something before all this?!

Members of families in which abuse was occurring often lived with the fear that someone might find out. By isolating the child emotionally as well as physically, the family severed the child's feelings of connection with the outside world, thus cutting off the child's ability to seek help from others. Another way to mitigate the problem was to threaten the child with further abuse, or worse:

> I told the minister. He wouldn't believe me and took no action. I told my aunt and she took no action. She said that he had abused her, also. I finally complained to my father, the perpetrator, and he said, "I own you, and there is no one who can stop me. I could kill you and no one would do anything. If you don't let me, I'll have to go to the little kids." His comments were most lethal.

Fear and Confusion

Mixed signals were common in the lives of these people as children. Many spoke of confusion between love and sex and between love and abuse. The children knew that mothers and fathers are supposed to take care of you and love you, but until they reached an age that they were exposed to other people and other families, they often accepted abuse as being normal; some even "thought it was love." Personalities of adults even seemed to change. When that happened, much confusion for the child resulted:

> My stepmom was very phony; she would be very kind when my dad was around. But when my dad was gone, she'd pull a knife out and chase me. I was not allowed to burp, smile, laugh, talk, or look at her. To me, she was a real devil, and I learned to trust no one. I grew up without running water. I would put kettled water into a wash basin to wash my face. Even though I knew what would happen, when I bent over to wash my face, then bang! My head is thrown on the floor, and she is dragging me by the hair. One night I accidentally burped, and she beat me up with a broom and left me on a dirt floor to sleep the night. My head was throbbing, and I prayed for death and, at age seven, I decided to commit suicide.

Bitterness, Anger, and Sorrow

Feelings of the "loss of a childhood" were often expressed by the participants, when they thought back to their earlier years: "I feel that I've missed out (and will never have) the 'normal' childhood that other people have had. I feel that I'll never trust the way other people do. I'm still missing a normal life, but then, what is a normal life?" Such feelings of loss generated considerable bitterness and anger:

> I remember my mother coming into my room swinging her arms, and I held my arms up to block her. I remember when I pulled a knife on my dad. I still cannot figure out why I wasn't killed. I was 13. I remember my friends asking me why my parents fought so much; they heard the fighting two blocks away. My mother slept with a whiskey bottle under her pillow. There are many more memories, too many for this paper. Today my feelings are out of anger and sorrow. If only they could have been helped, maybe they would be alive to see their grown kids and their grandkids.

Skepticism and Distrust

Loneliness and isolation; bitterness, anger, and sorrow; fear and confusion—these emotions occurring together, or in any combination, can cause a child to become skeptical and distrustful of everyone. Once the feelings have congealed, it is very difficult to convince children that adults in helping positions can be trusted with sharing secrets or searching for shelter. Some respondents indicated concerns that, if they told of the abuse, the family would be split up. Others felt that no one would believe them anyway. Some said that, as children, they found it very difficult to imagine their lives unfolding much differently than they already knew. Building trust is possible, but takes time and patience:

> I still distrust people. I find myself extremely selective in who I let know about me.

*   *   *

I spent ages five to sixteen bouncing from pillar to post; sometimes living with one parent and then the other; sometimes with only one of the stepparents, and not a parent at all; mostly just me. I always felt "in the way," nobody cared about me, mostly they were glad to get rid of me. I was told lots of lies and was very gullible, often trying to trust people and they usually "knifed me in the back."

*   *   *

Frankly, everything made me afraid. I did not trust anyone. I was afraid to. I was afraid at home, I was afraid at school. I was afraid almost everywhere most of the time. I was always angry. I had no one to trust.

Feeling Like I Might Go Crazy

We asked, in the vernacular, if there were times in their life related to the traumatic childhood experiences when the participants felt they were going "crazy." More than 75 percent answered yes to this question. Many of these participants had experienced sexual abuse. Coupled with feelings of distrust and isolation, survivors who experienced feelings of losing their mind often felt that "someone forgot to tell them something."

I often felt that I walked the edge between normal and insanity.

*   *   *

I thought I was crazy because no one else saw reality in my family like I did. I never felt crazy at school. School was safe. You used your intellect, not your emotions.

*   *   *

My mother tried to abort me. She loathed me as well as my father. Any problem or stress that she felt, she blamed on me. I was beaten with straps daily. I was never called by name. She would laugh at my fear of the dark, and would force me to walk with the lights out. I was locked in a dark closet with the mice for hours. If I touched her, she would throw me across the room and say, "Don't ever touch me!" My father was a fool. He allowed all this to go on and never protected me. He was sexually abusive also. My mother became very jealous. I tried to kill her when I was 14. I felt like I was going crazy often—and did—though no one seemed to recognize it. I just pretended I was sane.

Living in these kinds of situations could easily make a child feel terribly confused, even "crazy." As adults, the participants were more likely to have people to turn to for help, but as children they were most likely to be powerless and alone.

Guilt and Blame

Though children have little power in a chaotic family or one suffering severe stress, they often do not see it this way at all and take much of the responsibility for what is happening upon themselves:

> I experienced my father's degradation from the time my memories began until his death four years ago. The physical abuse only took place while I was smaller. Till this day, my mother reminds me that it is very bad to even think thoughts that question my father's goodness. The most difficult thing for me (and still is) was the endless hours of humiliation, particularly in front of my friends or other families. I was isolated on a small farm. I always believed (to some extent, I still do) that these terrible things were happening *because of me.*

One woman explained to us how she blamed her mother for many years for not protecting her from her alcoholic father's sexual abuse and violence. It was not until the father was dead, until the mother was old and frail, and the daughter was nearing middle age, that the daughter gained new insights into her mother's behavior:

> Mom told me, not long before she died, why she couldn't help me when father was raping me or beating me. Mom said that

when she was 8 or 9 years old her own father was abusing her, and he grabbed her pet cat by the tail and swung it as hard as he could into the outside wall of the house and killed it, and he said, "If you tell anyone, that's what I'm going to do to you!" Mom grew up and married my father. Mom said that every time my father was angry and abusive to us, it was like she became 8 years old again, and she would cower in silence and uncontrollable fear. After she told me this, I could understand better what was happening to us.

I went to visit her grave last week in Oregon. It was a kind of pilgrimage. We drove 1,500 miles to do this. I went with my best friend, because I could not go alone. I wept over her grave and told her I was sorry for what had happened to us together and that I did not blame her.

PEOPLE WHO HELPED

After studying the stories of the participants carefully, we have come to believe that the type of trauma the individual experienced was not the most critical issue. Rather, the alienation and fear of being alone or isolated from those who could give support was more devastating to the individuals. While studying the participants' responses, one is continually struck by how *alone* most of the participants felt. For example, 56 percent reported there was no one who would or could listen to them during this time; 20 percent said there was someone in the family; 9 percent cited teachers; 5 percent said friends; 3 percent checked "other"; 2 percent said professional counselors; no one cited clergy. If these children had found some sense of connection, support, and comfort in the world, perhaps it would have been more endurable for them, as they think back from their perspectives as adults.

Anger, violence, bitterness, distrust, depression, confusion, and chaos were all common themes in the stories the participants told us. And yet, even in the most strife-torn families, the individuals sometimes could find support. Forty-two percent of the participants indicated that other family members—sisters and brothers, mothers and fathers, aunts and uncles, grandparents—were important factors in their survival.

> As children we raised each other, discussing the problems and banding together to protect each other.

*   *   *

> I'm the oldest, and for punishment, I had to houseclean and baby sit. I would hold my brothers and sisters, feeling their warmth, their need for protection and safety. I taught them to be loving, not to hate like my stepmom.

*   *   *

> My aunt and uncle took me for the summer for several years. They got me away, showed me a normal family with love and kindness. If I could have just talked and explained what was happening, they might have understood.

*   *   *

> I would go to my grandma's a lot and she understood without my even explaining much of what happened. I often ran away to her house.

Friends also occasionally proved helpful:

> After we moved in with my father, he began sexually abusing me. This continued until I was 12. At that time, a new girlfriend began teaching me how to be assertive. I told her what happened and she taught me how to say NO! This was very different from the way I had been begging and pleading. He must have sensed the danger when I first said my "new word," because he backed off . . . then threatened to kill me if I ever told anyone about it. Even though the sexual abuse stopped, he continued to be physically, emotionally, and verbally abusive to me and my three brothers.

Others who were especially helpful included teachers and coaches. Professional counselors were rarely mentioned as being helpful in the traumatized child's life; though counselors played an important role in many individuals' adult life, they were mostly absent in their childhood. Clergy also were rarely mentioned—and only rarely in a positive light.

FACTORS THAT HELPED

How do individuals survive and transcend a traumatic childhood from their perspective as adults? Precisely what works? Generalizing, as we have warned before, is most difficult when talking about the wide variety of respondents' experiences. But we wish to begin our discussion of what helped by reemphasizing our finding that children only managed to survive, while some adults learned how to transcend. Children used whatever techniques and approaches they stumbled upon that seemed to work. In the long run, these approaches may have proved faulty, and negative unforeseen consequences were likely to result. But when experiencing traumatic stress, children and young adults often grabbed for anything they could reach. The following poem by one of the respondents summarizes what many, in essence, said about their childhoods:

> Twenty-five years, twenty-five years, twenty-five years,
> Oh, the tears, the tears, the fears
> Where was all the fun?
> I made myself numb
> I was quite dumb
> No one hears a silent cry
> So all I did was sigh
> And bury it all inside
> No one hears a silent cry.

Stating precisely what helped is difficult. Survival techniques children used, such as dissociation, selective amnesia, and denial, caused the immediate pain to subside, at least temporarily, and proved effective for many respondents in the short term. Being essentially powerless, they really had no other options. We chose to break down the key elements children used in the process of surviving and transcending into five areas: (1) spiritual resources, (2) dissociation, (3) escape, (4) accepting life as it is, and (5) survival by default.

Spiritual Resources

This coping strategy was the one most commonly used by the respondents. Religion or spirituality were mentioned by nearly everyone in the study, though beliefs and approaches were widely varied. The respondents recalled that as children they did not find spiritual leaders to be a source of help or comfort during their traumatic times. This seemed almost unanimous. Spirituality, however, which we will use here as a term much broader than institutionalized religion, was a powerful source of comfort for the traumatized children. "God," or "a higher being," gave a great amount of comfort and hope to those who felt they were forced to suffer in silence. Since they had no control over their lives as children, they could create a version of a higher power that was in control, one that had the traits of love and kindness or any other positive qualities they found to be in their own parents as caretakers:

> I always know that there is a place I can go and be fully accepted. I know that God will always love and forgive me.

> *   *   *

> I strongly believe in God and maybe this was from my upbringing, but I don't believe so much in the practice of the church.

References to angels were made in several stories. Guardian angels offered the protection and comfort that were so lacking in the world of the traumatized child:

> I believe that spiritual good exists and is available for us to tap in to. Sometimes it becomes manifest in angels—protectors, comforters. Bad things still happen, but we can connect with this good in ourselves, in nature, in others, and we can gain help and strength to survive. I felt somewhat protected, my soul was, but my body was not.

Although 56 percent of the respondents said they recalled having no person to talk to about their traumatic experience at the time it was occurring, most of them experienced a strong feeling of a higher power in control, and a better life ahead seemed to be the attitude that prevailed. Many described a personal relationship with God:

> Survival was somehow, somewhere, a belief in a loving God which was implanted in me. The most important factor in my survival and growth has been my faith in a loving Higher Power whose existence is evidenced to me through loving and caring adults with whom I have had relationships.

*   *   *

> God is always there to listen. What we wish is not necessarily what we get, but somehow or some way, we will later see what the reason was for what we went through.

As children, many of the respondents spent a great deal of time in prayer. Seventy percent said their religious beliefs were helpful to them as they grew through this difficult time in their life, but their views of organized religion varied markedly. In response to the question, "If you have been a member of an organized religious group, were members of this group helpful to you in dealing with these difficult times in your life?" 27.5 percent said yes, 63.7 percent said no, and 8.8 percent did not respond.

Many participants had changed their views on God and organized religion by the time they became adults. Some said they never really believed in a sheltering God (e.g., "If there was a God, he wouldn't let this happen to children"). Other relatively representative thoughts are reprinted here:

> I was raised a devout Lutheran. I was the "model," sang in the choir, and chaired the youth organization. I believe in God now, probably from my upbringing, but I don't believe in the practices of the church.

*   *   *

> I remember saying the words and thinking the beliefs were cor-
> rect. But one time as a very young girl, I was sitting in church
> thinking that this was such a farce. My mom, all prim and
> proper. We looked like a Norman Rockwell painting. But realis-
> tically, we're the family from hell. I just thought it was such a
> bunch of crap, and I always have. I was never confirmed. I am
> not a member of any church.

Negative attitudes about organized religion were common among
the respondents. On the other hand, personal spiritual belief systems
were very important for the individuals in the study, both as they remembered their thinking as children and their beliefs today as adults.
Human institutions proved ineffective at protecting the children from
trauma, so many developed their own relationship with the sacred in
life.

Dissociation

The adults in this study reported that, without the power to change
their world in positive ways, many of them as children learned how to
dissociate from the experience. This strategy is described vividly in
the following representative response:

> I learned to survive by letting myself go. I taught myself how to
> go numb, to have no feeling. I can feel myself floating out of my
> body and look down at a little girl screaming. I would fantasize
> that this is all a bad dream: A little dark-eyed girl sits in a big
> over-stuffed chair. She does not move or whimper, but prays that
> her mother will forget she is angry at her.

Escape

Many respondents told of how they escaped the nightmare of their
childhood by disappearing into books, finding goodness in nature,
focusing on schoolwork and school activities, or working hard to become really good at something:

I am a dreamer, an avid reader. I got lost in stories, books, fantasies.

* * *

To survive, I learned to be quiet and good, and also invisible. I found places outside the home to get my needs fulfilled. Church, school, campfire, anything that got me out of the house. Being in nature, riding bikes, I learned to see and enjoy the beauty around me, and not dwell on the negative.

* * *

I discovered at age five that I was smart. I learned to read before I started school. The self-confidence I had kept me going many years. If I doubted myself in some areas, I could prove myself on an intellectual level. School was my haven, my escape. My tears were released while crying for the characters in books I read. Books were my friends.

Accepting Life As It Is

As children with no power or control over the situation, many simply accepted the life they were living because there was no other reality for them. When asked if they viewed these events as traumatic at the time, 47 percent of the respondents said no. Their explanations for this response varied but was generally explained by the fact that they had limited experience in life and no other perspective from which to view their situation:

I was so busy trying to survive the hellish situation that it didn't clearly register how traumatic the events were. Every day was traumatic!

* * *

I accepted abuse as normal at the time. I thought [sexual] abuse was love.

Many of the participants as children apparently accepted their fate because they had no visions of a better world. Then, as they grew into adolescence, they began to see that all families were not like theirs. Many recalled, at this point in life, developing what may seem to the outsider to be a relatively cold, clear-eyed view of reality. "How did you survive all this?" the outsider might ask. The insider might answer, "What choice did I have? To live the life I was powerless to change, or die."

Genuine help for the children in these situations was not there. The world was apparently looking it in the other way.

Survival by Default

In adulthood, many individuals picked up the pieces of their lives in a steady, methodical, rational manner, which provides a good definition of transcendence. But these same individuals' memories of their traumatic childhood present a completely different picture. The child that the adult remembers was not well developed cognitively, socially, or emotionally and was often overwhelmed by the traumatic experiences swirling around her or him. They somehow managed to survive it all, sometimes in terror, sometimes in bewilderment, sometimes in a trance.

The participants survived childhood trauma almost by default. Pure luck, or what one might call a strange twist of fate, rescued them, literally, from a brutal death:

> When I was between three or four years old, my father took a large butcher knife and tried to kill me in the closet of his and mother's bedroom. I was terrified. I backed into the closet to get away from him. He must have chased me there. I backed in and fell into a box, and I couldn't get out. He came at me, and then someone opened the back door to the house and called my father's name. Again the person called, and my dad backed out of the closet and took me by the hand and gave me a hug. I remember that I couldn't understand why he did that terrible thing to me and then hugged me. I don't even remember who came to the back door. It could have been the neighbor, but maybe it was mother. Dad hid the knife behind, like down the side of his pants, not inside, but kind of in the back of him, next to his pants

leg, and went into the kitchen. I think he put the knife in the sink. I don't know where I went. I know that person played a part in my life that day.

CONCLUSION

When the abuse was occurring, the fortunate survived. The best term we can find for what they did in childhood is *endured*, which implies to us that they simply got through it as best they could. The dictionary says it means, among other things, to carry on through, despite hardships; to bear with tolerance; to continue in existence; to remain; to last; to hold out. Sometimes as we are puzzled over the right terms to explain what happened to these people as children, we found ourselves entertaining the term *muddled*. The chilling word pictures many of these individuals painted of themselves as children suggest that they simply floundered. Using the analogy of a sinking ship, they grasped at anything they could when they had the capacity and strength to grasp, bobbing up on occasion, sinking on occasion. As children they simply muddled through. They had little ability to rationally manage their lives—and almost no power.

We might also wonder why they did not give up. What made them hold on for something better? As children with limited cognitive abilities, why did they keep reaching for lifeboats? Was it the human spirit? Was it the innate urge, which exists in each of us, for their inner spirit to be free—to be free of the abuse and trauma that was happening to them?

My dad was crazy. He made us kids weird.
Things were definitely not as they appeared.
Dad gave up drinkin' when he did marry,
But with him, his past he sure did carry.

He cussed and swore, he ran us kids in the ground.
'Til his voice we'd hear was not a good sound.
We'd shudder and shake and wonder, "What's wrong?"
His words struck deep as if with a prong.

We were robbed. We were raped. We were beaten blue.
We thought we were so bad, this was our due.
With self-esteem sagging and spirits 'bout dead,
We'd try to function with a feeling of dread.

We are angry. We are upset and downright pissed.
To think of all the good things we missed.
He took away our childhood, our hopes, our dreams.
And now we ask, "Why are we coming apart at the seams?"
It's only a half-century later, we came to see
He had no right to take away "Me."
I know I'm special, I'm wonderful, and I'm full of spunk.
Therefore, I know that I am not sunk.

God made me beautiful, inside and out.
That's what it's really all about.
When the wounds heal a little, I will forgive.
Then only, as a whole person, will I truly live.
(The pain, the pain, I wish you knew
You gave to me, dad, without a clue.)

The missing ingredient was love. It was there,
But never shown.

I love you, dad. I wish you could tell
me that. How much I need to hear it.

Chapter 3

Transcending As Adults

When we were searching for the participants in our study, we tried to make it clear that we were looking for people who had both survived and transcended a traumatic childhood. After participating in the process of completing the questionnaire, 83 percent concluded that they had, indeed, survived *and* transcended, 6 percent did not answer the question, and 11 percent said they had only survived.

Even though this was a group of people who generally felt they were doing well in life as adults, they still felt the impact of their childhood traumas. Seventy-two percent said they still experienced personal guilt associated with what had happened in their lives. Many had learned through counseling and by their own observations that they were not to blame because they were only children when the trauma happened, but the experience still remained very painful. This was true for those who were sexually abused, especially for some whose mothers had allegedly blamed them for tempting the perpetrators.

Seventy-three percent of the respondents said that the traumatic experiences as children had made them better people. "All things considered," we asked them, "how do you see this event affecting your life in the final analysis?" Sixty-four percent said that the effects were a combination of both negative and positive; 23 percent said all positive, and 13 percent said all negative. When asked, "How do you know you're really okay today?" most said, in effect, that they were alive, able to function in the world, and continuing on in the process of transcending.

Surviving and Transcending a Traumatic Childhood
© 2007 by The Haworth Press, Inc. All rights reserved.
doi:10.1300/5839_03

We were interested in the strengths that each respondent saw in their family of origin today, for we wanted to see if the participants saw positive changes over time. The majority said their family of origin had "no strengths" today. Scattered responses focused on "a family member who is supportive," "a strong work ethic" in the family of origin today, and "my mother's organizational ability." "Structure" and "rigidity" were also listed as strengths, but for the most part, families of origin were not seen as particularly healthy.

Fifty percent of the participants had attended support group meetings as adults in order to help themselves heal from their experiences. Eighty-three percent developed hobbies, skills, interests, or other ways to spend time that related to their difficult life experiences. What served as a method of coping as a child further developed into healthy activities for many as adults. Reading, art, music, and poetry were noted most often.

Nearly three-fourths of the participants in the study had children (74.7 percent). Even though many of the accounts of the survivors who became parents were positive, the carryover of the traumatic abuse some suffered was still present. One of the final questions we asked was whether or not they worried about falling into a vicious cycle of abuse and passing on the pain and disorder they experienced in their families of origin to their own children. Forty percent said they did worry about intergenerational transmission of past problems, while 56 percent said they were not worried. A few chose not to have children at all. As one woman said, "I didn't want to have kids because I was afraid they'd grow up like I did—that I wouldn't be a good parent, so I was afraid to have kids."

The statistics revealed many strengths of the participants. Even with the fears and phobias, the flashbacks and dreams, there is an ongoing sense of transcending by the majority of the respondents. These individuals are in the process of transcending now, and they commonly believe they will continue to deal with the issues surrounding the trauma for the rest of their lives. The picture is very, very complex.

Part of the complexity of transcending has to do with dealing with the trauma throughout one's life. It is never over. The work is never done. We asked the question, "What still hurts today?" Nearly everyone had an answer:

It still hurts to see my father treat my mother disrespectfully. He is chronically angry/explosive. I still get scared when I see this, as it conjures up the horrible scenes of my childhood. It would be nice to be able to walk away from it.

*   *   *

It still hurts to realize that my parents do not love me, and never did love me. I can allow myself to deal with the pain, feel it, and share it with others. It lasts a shorter period of time.

*   *   *

I have still not resolved all the issues related to my traumatic childhood. I'm working on the reservoir of pain that exists. I will succeed in getting rid of it, as I have prevailed on other issues. I am not in pain, but there exists pain in my heart. This is a big difference. Perhaps it will never leave. I'll just learn to accept that.

*   *   *

It has been 30 years since the difficult time in my life. The overt sexual abuse stopped at 16, but the implied threat continued for years and, actually, I am not going to be sure the threat is over until he is dead or I am.

When did individuals move from the child's perspective to the adult perspective? When did they move from simply surviving to transcending? When did this developmental process take place? How did it happen? Each story is different, but, generally speaking, this happened when they became free enough to distance themselves emotionally and physically from the source of their trauma. They had also reached the point where they had acquired the power that comes with being an adult and could actually limit their exposure to the trauma. They could also cognitively reflect on what had happened and begin to do things that helped them heal. For some this began when they were young adults, and for others it did not begin until years later. Here is a sampling of how some participants came to the realization that they were now in control of their lives:

> I have realized that when I was a child, I couldn't control what happened. The adults should have controlled that. I am now an adult and in control of what hurts and what makes me happy. I choose to be happy.

> * * *

> The key person is me. In some ways I was fortunate to learn to rely on myself. I knew I had to make the change. No one else could do it for me. I went through a long, difficult period in my adult life, and I didn't know how to make it better or if that was possible. We need to believe that it can change before we're willing to do anything about it.

> * * *

> Surviving is just making it. I did that. Transcending is putting everything in perspective, understanding it, and accepting it as part of your life but not letting it rule your life.

As we read the stories of the ninety participants, we concluded that transcending was a very long, difficult, and painful process. Although one may become what is considered a healthy adult, the trauma and the effects of the trauma never completely go away. The trauma or abuse will always be the dark thread in the tapestry. Even though it will be less visible, less pervasive, it will always be part of the fabric of one's life. These individuals were saying that they had to do for themselves. As the woman said, "The key person is me." Individuals transcended because *they* made it happen.

Knowing that each individual had to make it with motivation from within, there were things that, looking back, these adults identified that helped them in the process of transcending. Some of the things were deliberately planned, such as a woman who knew she had to get an education to be free of her parents. Or the person who said she wanted to get married and was very deliberate about creating a life for her family that was different from her own experience growing up.

Other times, they were in so much pain that they just knew they had to move forward, not knowing exactly what would come next. For example, a woman reflecting on being a young adult knew she had to get out of the house where the abuse was occurring or she would die. She had no idea how she would make it on her own, but she had more personal resources just because she was an adult. The individuals almost intuitively turned to spirituality as a source of help, because without it they did not feel they would be able to move on to further healing. We have the sense that if we talked with people during these very difficult times of healing they would not be able to clearly articulate what was helping and why. However, as people who have moved to a fairly healthy place in life, they could reflect on their past and tell us what helped and why it had been useful in the long process of transcending.

The participants in the study identified five things that they felt helped them transcend a traumatic childhood during their adult years. The things talked about most often by the participants were spirituality, therapy and/or support groups, getting married, escaping from the abuse, and looking forward not back.

SPIRITUALITY

Every respondent was affected by religion and/or spirituality as they moved through the process of transcending. For some, religion was a positive factor in transcending the trauma; for most it was not. Although 70 percent said religious or spiritual beliefs were helpful to them as they moved along the process of transcending, 64 percent said organized religion had not been helpful in dealing with their difficult times.

When participants in this study talked about religion they usually talked about it as an organized belief system involving God that included involvement in a faith community or congregation. Religion for the participants in this study was going to church on Sunday mornings and sometimes attending other events during the week. As children, a few participants had also attended church schools, which were affiliated with a congregation. Participants talked about spirituality, on the other hand, as having a personal relationship with a higher being, usually referred to as God.

In this book, we will be true to our data in that we will report the findings as the participants described their experiences of church. We know, however, that many who are reading this book may meet in a mosque or a temple or some other place of worship to practice religious beliefs. We hope that the readers know that those places are important in the practice of some religions, but they were not talked about in this study.

We have already described in Chapter 2 how spirituality was helpful for children as they survived the trauma, and how organized religion turned them away when they asked for help. There were several individuals who had gone to religious leaders asking for help to get away from the abuse. Generally, the religious leaders would tell them there was nothing they could do. Their father was an elder or held some other position in the church that made it impossible for the religious leader to intervene. The children were also told that the church leaders could not interfere with their family's personal life. Religious beliefs were also used as a rationale for parents, religious leaders, and teachers to abuse them. These people were in positions of authority, and they often used religious teaching to justify their authority over children. Children went to a place of worship Sunday after Sunday hearing how they were supposed to live their lives, with their parents acting like fine, upstanding religious people. Yet, the children experienced beatings afterward while they were still in their church clothes. Many turned to something else for comfort and support. They turned to spirituality.

As adults they turned away from religion because their experience was that religious leaders, congregational members, and the abusers who were involved with the religious organization had not helped them as children:

> I do not attend church. Abused religiously—I stopped speaking with my father when he told me that the Bible says that he has the right to do what he wanted to me—that I have no rights, but only duties, that I must honor and obey him no matter what.

*   *   *

> There was emotional abuse in church and the leader said Dad had a duty to spank us. I lost my naive belief in Jesus and God.

It took me 22 years to rediscover God and a belief system. I am still searching for more spiritual growth.

* * *

My family was a strict Norwegian Lutheran family—we went to church, Sunday school, fellowship, and choir. I knew there was a God—I was terrified of Him. I wanted to die, but I knew Satan would get my soul and I'd be damned in hell for all eternity. My religious beliefs have changed. I know God is loving, not hateful.

* * *

I loathe "religion," yet have deep spiritual beliefs. Being Catholic was a torture. I was told daily by sadistic, ignorant nuns that my father had to go to hell—and me also, because I would sneak off with him to the Protestant church. I could not trust or believe any of the adults in my life, so I had to fantasize a lot, making my own God.

* * *

My religious faith changed because it showed that my parents' religion was crazy, and I had to develop my own. I learned that the Catholic religion is based on guilt, much like the relationship I had with my stepmother and father.

Spirituality became a source of comfort and love after the hard times. It helped them through the difficult times of healing as an adult:

I have a higher power that helps me get through the difficult times. My current spiritual beliefs give me faith that I will be taken care of, regardless of my current reality.

Becoming spiritual was a developmental process in itself (Skogrand, Singh, Allgood, DeFrain, DeFrain, & Jones, 2005). It seemed that spirituality was at first a source of comfort and a way to get through the difficult times. As they progressed through the healing process they talked about spirituality helping them to understand what had happened to them and to think about their suffering in new ways:

> Through prayer one does not feel alone. It made me understand that God sometimes shows a bad thing to make you see the good better. God has plans for me to keep going through life. I know ours is a loving God and there is a reason for everything that happens.

*   *   *

> I came to accept my higher power and to trust in my understanding of salvation. People do the best they can with what they have to work with. In God's eyes I am as sinful as my parents, so I do not judge them more harshly. I have a purpose beyond ordinary experience, somewhat detached from the trappings of success.

Some participants talked about their spiritual life as being a contributing factor in having a sense of peace with what had happened to them and understanding why it happened. It helped them to go beyond themselves to helping others:

> My relationship with my higher power is a personal one. Belief in a higher power was essential to my healing process. I had to understand why this would happen to me, what I had done to deserve it. I felt there had to be a purpose to it; that at least it strengthened me and maybe I could help someone some day.

*   *   *

> My "inner child" and I have a great relationship, as do my "higher self" and I. I have taken the trip deep into the unknown, fully prepared with the tools to transcend the experience and glean the wisdom and return to myself the power lost as I gathered the shattered pieces of my soul. I brought clarity to who I am, why I am the way I am, and how blessed I am to have risked knowing a trusted God to carry me through. I have grown so

strong in my own truth that I can now share this without the pain and devastation that once overwhelmed me.

Spirituality gave adults the opportunity to develop their own understanding of God, one that was not limited to the boundaries of a religious denomination and one that was beyond the understanding of children. This woman sums up her understanding of spirituality and describes how it helped her in the process of transcending:

> My faith in a personal higher power is rooted in a personal choice rather than a child's acceptance of what adults around her tell her is true. My spirituality has always been very quiet, very personal. I do not believe that God sends us trials; I believe that there is a force of evil—call it *the devil* or anything you like—and that man has *free will*. God is available to us always, manifesting Himself through loving people and beauty in the world around us. There are good things that can be learned or gained through even the most horrific events.

THERAPY AND/OR SUPPORT GROUPS

Sixty-four percent of the participants in this study indicated that they had sought the guidance of a therapist who helped them in the process of transcending. They usually went to a therapist only after they had become very desperate, unable to address the pain, sadness, lack of sleep, nightmares, or depression. Often, they did not know what was causing the symptoms and understood only after they began seeing a therapist. We also learned that 36 percent did not seek the help of a therapist in transcending their traumatic childhoods. Some were proud of the fact that they had done it on their own.

We also found that 51 percent of the participants attended a support group in the process of transcending. On average, they attended twenty-six meetings as part of the healing process. Some saw a therapist and attended support group meetings. Others only saw a therapist or attended support group meetings, but not both.

Participants in the study gave numerous indications that what happened to them resulted in mental and psychological stress that might be alleviated by therapy or attending a support group. Seventy-six percent indicated they felt "they were going to go crazy" at times in their life. Sixty-nine percent indicated they, at some point, "had wanted to go to sleep and wake up after the pain had gone away." Thirty-four percent had "given themselves physical pain on purpose" to take the emotional pain away. Fifty-seven percent had thought about committing suicide because of what had happened to them. Nineteen percent had actually tried to kill themselves at some point. These are understandable mental health symptoms of the trauma experienced by those who participated in the study.

Although a majority of participants in this study sought the help of a therapist and attended a support group, many did not tell us very much about the experience. Some participants told us why they went to a therapist and how they benefited. Others talked about the length of time that it took to heal even with the help of a therapist.

One of the stories described how therapy helped a man who completed his questionnaire in prison, where he was serving a seventy-two-year sentence. He was abused by an aunt and uncle, a coach, and nuns at school. He finally received counseling while in prison. He indicated that, until he received counseling, he never really understood what had happened to him.

A thirty-nine-year-old woman who was sexually abused by a variety of family members, including two uncles and an older sister, began to see a counselor after she got married. She had been having nightmares, suffered with insomnia, and thought she was going crazy. A counselor helped her remember the abuse that she had blocked out and helped her through numerous bouts of depression. She had been going to counseling for three years and participating in support groups. She said:

> My counselor helped me dig into my past with kindness and understanding. By going through a lot of painful memories, I got it out into the open. . . . Mainly, I went so I could learn to trust people and learn how to deal with what happened to me.

A man had this to say about how a psychologist helped him:

> Transcending, I believe, is an ongoing process. I first had to remember all I could about the abuse I endured and have help from the psychologist to put it into place and then work on for-

giving those who abused me. The absolute hatred I had was tearing me apart. As I have worked on forgiving these people I have found this wonderful person, ME.

One woman added, "I believe I owe my psychologist my life. She helped me transcend the most difficult period of my life.
Others had this to say:

> I've heard some people say that they didn't need a stranger to help them—that they could do it alone. I needed help, help to raise my self-esteem and to let go of the past. This past year in therapy I've learned to stop trying to control the future. I live in this moment. . . . Counseling has also taught me that it's okay to let people see the real you. I don't have to pretend to be someone else to be loved.

*   *   *

> At first I went [to a counselor] because I was desperate. Later, I went because I needed to know about myself and my family."

One woman described the long process of working with a therapist to address the multiple personalities which developed during her childhood. Her first memory of abuse was of sexual abuse by her father at age three. She was also physically abused by her mother. This woman felt that therapy, and later meditation, was the key in surviving and transcending her traumatic childhood:

> I saw a therapist for two years and she helped me find joy in my life. . . . She saved my life. . . . She let the three kids (my personalities) have "turns" in the sessions so they could be heard and let me know what they wanted. Through modeling, having me remember parenting my real kids, she taught me to nurture my "inside" kids. She taught me trust and love. After two years of therapy, she introduced me to a meditation group. This has brought peace, love, and joy into my life. Most of my anger is gone. My dad is dead, but in meditation I forgave him. I also forgave my mom. This has helped me find peace. I'm studying to be a healer and I believe my childhood was a gift to me. I work

with light, love, and energy. I do not judge others. I love myself and others. I found myself; it all must start there. No one else can make you happy. Only I can make myself happy, and I am. I am finally at peace and not suicidal, which I was in the past.

The healing process, even with the help of a therapist, was very slow. One woman indicated that she had been in therapy intermittently for twenty-one years. Another woman said, "I have been in therapy for over twenty years, off and on. . . . I went into therapy to keep from repeating my parents' bad behaviors with my own children." This woman went on to say:

Sometimes I get really angry with God because I am 60 years old and I am still in therapy. I think that I could have done so much with the time, money and energy that I have needed to learn about myself and cope with the damage I experienced. But then I look at how much my getting better has helped a lot of other people and I feel I do Christ's work. . . . Struggle is worth it. Things that come easily are not as valuable.

Participants also described how support groups helped them transcend. They talked about what the groups did for them:

When other women had discussed their pain, it triggered emotional responses within myself. . . . It got in touch with some factor of my childhood experience and I was able to gain insight into why I think the way I do and why I react to violence and, maybe, even how I learned to cope.

* * *

I went to counselors because I needed help and I knew I had to get some help in order to survive. It always helps me to talk to someone about my situation. The support groups all helped me to understand that I was not crazy and there were other people who had lived through the same experiences.

* * *

I went to support groups to release the shame where it was safe to do so.

Finally, one man who attended Alcoholics Anonymous weekly described how it helped him. He said, "Without AA I would be dead."

GETTING MARRIED

It was clear as we read the testimonies of the participants that what happened to them as children affected every aspect of their adult life, including their thoughts about marriage. In fact, 70 percent of those who participated in our study said their childhood experiences affected their decision to be involved in a committed relationship or to marry. For some, it meant that they were afraid to trust another person; for others, it meant they wanted a happy marriage and family life because they had not experienced a good family life as a child.

Out of the ninety participants, eighty-four (93 percent) had been married at least once. Of those who that had been married at least once, 49 percent felt that marriage was helpful in transcending their traumatic childhoods. Some found this help in their first marriage, and some found it in a subsequent marriage. On average, participants in this study were married 1.3 times. We will describe how participants talked about both the unhappy and the happy marriages that were part of their life experiences.

Many of the participants had unhealthy role models when it came to marriage. Therefore, they did not always make good choices about marriage or did not have relationship skills that were likely to result in happy marriages. Some went "from the frying pan into the fire," as marriage provided a way for them to get away from the abusive situation only to be abused by a spouse.

Bad Marriages

Many of the respondents (42 percent) who had been married at least once experienced a bad marriage relationship. Some went on to find helpful and supportive marriage relationships later. Some continued to live in a dysfunctional relationship, or even went on to one or more subsequently bad relationships. Of those who experienced a bad relationship at some time, 57 percent were abused by their spouse. These were all women whose husbands verbally, physically, or sexually abused them. Some of the more severe cases of abuse were as bad as what they experienced during their traumatic childhood. Here are examples of three women's marriage experiences:

> He was very volatile. I spent years looking down the barrel of a .45, was thrown across rooms, and threatened. I finally had enough and felt my children's safety was at stake. One was 18 months and the other was 3 years. I packed the kids in the car and crossed state lines in the middle of the night. I left the house, appliances, and furniture, and started from scratch.

*   *   *

> He beat me regularly, raped me regularly, and tortured me in several ways. He would make me do things I didn't want to do. He used to take me in a car or on a motorcycle and would drive like a maniac over lawns, over street signs, as much as 70-80 miles per hour. He cheated on me, broke my nose. At age 21 I left him and moved to another state. Then I married a recovering alcoholic and am leading a fairly normal life.

*   *   *

> I got pregnant at 21 and married the man. He was the first and I thought he loved me and I him. He was abusive—mentally at first and then physically. Once he nearly cut my throat and once he tore up all our clothes because I didn't iron them right. He'd go out Friday and return Monday. I didn't sleep because I was afraid to be alone. When I was 29 he left me for another woman. He threatened that if I didn't give him a divorce he'd disappear one day with one of the kids.

One woman described her husband as abusive, but also described her own behavior as harmful to their relationship. Eventually she found happiness in a marriage and through faith in God:

> I got married because I was afraid of being alone. He blamed me for six years for his failures and insisted I be involved with him in sexual "swinging." I drank heavily at parties, flirted with oth-

ers, but was not involved with others beyond petting during the marriage. I got divorced. I was scared to be alone. I continued to drink heavily, had numerous affairs with married men—men I picked up at bars, boyfriends of women I called friends—and continued to work full-time as a social worker. Then I met my current husband who picked me up at a bar. He was 15 years older than me—it didn't look promising. He was extremely intelligent. We became involved at his insistence in sexual swinging. He met someone else but we got back together again. I realized I wanted to find peace and began to pray to an unknown God. We got married a year later and are now conservative Catholics. We moved to a small town. We have stayed sober and we love our life.

One woman had been married fifty-one years to a man who was an alcoholic and was verbally and sexually abusive. He was Catholic and she believed that marrying a Catholic man would be her key to happiness, but it was not. Even though she has "never experienced peace of mind in seventy-four years of life," she stayed married.

Other participants were married to spouses who were abusive, but they described the abuse as being less severe than what they experienced growing up. One woman said, "I married a drunk and he called me a bitch and a whore. I knew I really was one because of what I let happen." Another woman stayed married to a man for forty-four years and raised seven children with him. Her husband disparaged her because of her childhood.

Of those who had bad marriage experiences, some described their marriages as not being good, but did not indicate that there was abuse. Examples of these types of marriage experiences included the spouse "being addicted," "an alcoholic work addict," and "untrustworthy with my feelings." One woman described her unhappy marriage this way:

I got married at 18 and he was not a wonderful, religious man. I thought he would take care of me. What a joke that was. The farm economy went to pot and it was always my fault, so I went and got a job. Now he tells everyone I don't do anything at home. After 35 years I thought it would get better.

Marriages That Were Supportive

Here is one person's story about what she was looking for as she entered adulthood and left the family where the trauma occurred. This story is an example of how a person survived trauma, looked for a spouse and a family that would be better than the family she came from, and moved through the process of transcending with the help of her husband:

> For the first 17 years of my life all I can remember is constant fighting, it never ended. We never had a phone because my dad would rip it out of the wall when my mom would use it to call the cops. I remember my dad constantly getting us kids out of bed in the middle of the night to yell at us about our mother being a whore. He'd continue his accusations until she'd come home about two in the morning. They would have a knock-down-drag-out fight. I remember my father beating my mom and my mom breaking whatever she could get hold of over his head: guns, toys, vacuum cleaners, anything.
>
> Being the oldest of five, I was constantly held responsible for whatever happened, so I had a lot of personal guilt. I was told by mom, who also let us know that she never wanted us, that we were to blame for our father's drinking problem. She also had her problems with alcohol. She slept with a whiskey bottle under her mattress.
>
> I remember a fight with my dad where I pulled a knife on him to kill him. I still can't figure out why I wasn't killed. I was 13.
>
> A dream I had as a child was of a beautiful guy coming to rescue me. Fortunately, it happened. Marriage to me was, in some ways, an escape. But, finally, my life did get better. My parents died when I was 17 and I married my wonderful husband shortly thereafter. We've been married ever since. It is the only close relationship I have ever had. We have two children, eight and five years of age, and I love them all the more because of my childhood experiences and never let them think they aren't wanted.

My childhood has made me stronger emotionally. I don't break down. I sometimes feel I create chaos unintentionally in my life to distract myself from the emotional pain. When my husband says something, I think about it and realize what I'm doing and try hard to stop.

A caring person who gives support through difficult times can provide a traumatized person with the courage and ability to move to a better place. Nearly half of the participants in this study believed they found a spouse who was helpful in the process of transcending. Some of the adults in this study described specific things their spouses did to help them transcend. Others described their spouse as someone who was not particularly supportive but who did not do the bad things they had experienced in their childhoods.

Of those who said their spouses positively affected their ability to transcend, 46 percent described specific helpful things their spouses did. These adults reported having a spouse who listened, loved unconditionally, were not judgmental, and were nurturing. Their spouses would listen to them talk about their pain:

> [He] took the time, almost three years, to listen and help me deal with my life. He helped me by talking to me and digging into my past with kindness and understanding. My husband tried to help with his understanding, because he wanted me to be happy and he thought my family was very fucked up because of the things they let happen. I wasn't close to anyone until I met my husband.

The spouse was often the first person who was entrusted with information about the difficult family life and abuse:

> When I first met my husband I was ashamed to have him visit my home, because I was afraid he'd find out about my dad's alcoholism. I had been afraid to tell any friends and rarely had people over because of this. Somehow I got the courage to tell him about my dad's problem, and my husband never cast any judgment. He is even cordial toward my dad. We've been married 17 years now and I appreciate my husband even more now

than when we first got married. He's a supportive husband, who loves me unconditionally.

*   *   *

The first person I was ever able to tell was my husband, [who was] then my fiancé. I was afraid he might not marry me when he knew about the emotional abuse, but he looked on it as a challenge.

Several people talked about how their spouses helped them recover by letting them know that they were loved and accepted. In most cases this was not something they had previously experienced. One woman described her husband's support when she was going through a very difficult time in this way:

I said, "Honey, don't leave me alone." He'd even go to the bathroom with me. He'd hold me. One of those bad sessions lasted three days. He never left my side.

This woman added that her husband was always a person with whom she could talk. Others described their spouses' role in helping them transcend:

[When I felt like I was going crazy] my husband helped me realize that things weren't as bad as I thought they were. . . . I married "Mr. Right." My husband often tells me that he is proud of my accomplishments.

*   *   *

[A key factor in surviving and transcending] was my wonderful husband of 53 years. He made me feel important. My husband and I have helped many hurting people.

*   *   *

Luckily, I married a boy who grew up to be a wonderful, sensitive man. . . .Without his loving support I may never have outgrown trying to be good at the expense of being myself. I was attracted at an early age (16) to my husband who wants to live peacefully, and does; and he knows how to love.

Another person said, "My husband has been wonderful. I have shared everything with him and he *still* loves me."

Other adults who transcended traumatic childhoods described their spouses as taking control and being very deliberate at doing things that the respondent viewed as being helpful in the process of transcending. One person said her spouse "got me into Al Anon." Another woman said:

> My husband detested my mother for what she did to me. When I started behaving in some ways that reminded me of mother, my husband and my medical doctor found a very good psychiatrist for me. My husband was one of the key people who helped me in surviving and transcending.

Another spouse actually showed his wife how to stop taking the abuse:

> My husband would condemn my parents' behavior. If I got very upset while on the phone, he'd grab it out of my hands and hang up. Eventually I learned to hang up myself. Eventually my mom got the hint when I told her to back off and meant it.

Two participants added, "[My spouse] helped me realize I was okay and my parents were the sick people," and, "My husband was a constant reality check on what was important and what was trivial."

Some respondents were able to tell us how their marriage and resulting family life fit together to help them transcend:

> I am close to my foster parents, my wife's parents, and my two kids. I cannot imagine life without my wife. I feel positive and happy most of the time. I know my wife loves me. I am married to a tolerant, wonderful woman. I have absolute faith in her love. I believe that she and our relationship tell the story of how I was able to transcend a childhood of abuse and neglect. She is my best friend.

Some of the respondents described how their spouses were helpful in transcending, because the spouses did not do abusive things. It is apparent that, for some, expectations were not very high. In some cases, they indicated that there was no love, but married life with their spouse was better than anything they had experienced in the past. A woman who later came to believe that she was lesbian said, "I was not physically attracted to him, but he was kind and he offered me refuge." Other responses indicated life was not great, but was better than their previous life experiences:

> He was honest and had a steady job. He wasn't a heavy drinker. I have a nice husband. One reason I was attracted to my husband was that he and his family are very natural about their sexual selves and very comfortable about it.

> *   *   *

> I did fall into a pattern as a young adult of getting into abusive relationships. Now I won't tolerate being abused, and have a good, non-abusive relationship.

Marriage played a role in the process of transcending for many of the participants in this study. For some it was positive and for others it was not. Some said that, even though the marriage was not very good, it got them out of the abusive situation—it was the first step in the long process of transcending. Sometimes the marriages were good and their spouses actually were major contributors to the process of transcending. These participants were able to have good marriages and family lives, and appreciated a very different life than the one they had in their childhood.

ESCAPING FROM THE ABUSE

For many, moving away came when they were eighteen years old as they went off to college, work, or to the military. Even though we did not specifically ask the participants if moving away was a way to transcend a traumatic childhood, 44 percent of the participants in the study *volunteered* that moving away and/or severing contact was a critical part of transcending.

Moving away from one's family is not unusual since most people do that as they look forward to building their own lives. Generally, young adults are able to begin using the skills they learned growing up as they try new things and look forward, relying on the foundation their families provided when they were children. There is often continued support from parents as they begin their journey as adults. Many who participated in this study, however, talked about moving away as a relief, an escape, because they were moving to a place without abuse or trauma. In most cases, participants did not expect support from their families. Instead, they often went into the world with fears about what life had to hold and were ill-prepared emotionally, socially, and financially. They saw the move, however, as a more positive alternative than continuing to stay where the abuse could continue.

The stories of how participants moved away and/or severed ties with their abusers took many forms. For example, one fifty-six-year-old woman lived in orphanages and twenty different foster homes in Hungary until she was thirteen years old, at which time her birth parents came to get her. In foster care she was forced to work for long hours with little food to eat and no affection. Living with her birth parents did not make things better. Her parents were both deaf and were very poor and they all slept in one bed. Her father was an alcoholic and beat both her and her mother. After a year she chose to go back to the orphanage rather than continue to live with the abuse in her home.

Moving back to the orphanage was the beginning of her process of moving away from the trauma in her childhood. She stayed in the orphanage until she was fifteen when it was expected the she get a job and take care for herself. Her life was very difficult as she worked for a construction company carrying cement nine hours per day and barely earning enough money to live. As a young adult she survived the Hungarian Revolution and, at age twenty-one, was able to immigrate to the United States. At that point her life began to improve.

Planning Began at a Young Age

Some participants described how they had made plans for years to get away from the abuse. One woman described her plans to leave home this way:

By the time I was in my second year of high school, I had my plan completely formulated. I was determined to graduate from high school, go to some kind of vocational school, and leave my family behind. My plans were to leave my home town, change my name, and never look back. I was still too young to know that you can run, but you can never hide from where you came.

She hinted at how difficult it was to follow through with such plans. For some, it took several years to reach their goal because they had so little support.

Another woman also described how, as a child, she began planning to get out on her own: "I knew that if I could support myself and get out of the house, I would survive. I did what I had to do to make this happen with education."

Creating a New Life

Several participants in the study left home to find work or go to school, not knowing how or if they would be able to make it on their own. It was common for individuals in the study to leave home at seventeen or eighteen years of age to find something better. One woman described how she did this, but was completely on her own:

From 17 to 20 years of age I attended nursing school away from my parents. I lived in the dorm and being away from my parents helped, but I really had no support.

One woman described how she moved into an apartment with friends and how her friends became her family:

For the first few months away from home, I stayed at friends' houses with their families. . . . During the last year of high school I had my own apartment and was continually making friends. . . . [I began] to transcend when I finally moved away from both parents. I had a support group of friends. They were friends who I told my home-life stories to. It made me realize how fucked up my [divorced] parents were. The sister closest to my age had a boyfriend who helped her deal with stuff and together they moved into a new apartment. Both of them helped me tremendously because they had gone through the same treatment from my folks. My roommates became my family.

Another woman also said that one of the things that happened to make things better was that she moved away from both of her parents who were divorced:

> I left my parents' homes at 18 without any financial or emotional support. I knew from a young age that I could only depend on myself. I worked my way through college, traveled all over the world, met interesting people and married a European.

Other participants in the study chose a variety of avenues of escape. One woman entered a convent at seventeen because she "was too scared to face the 'real world.'" She spent nine years there where she grew by learning how to discipline herself.

Some men enlisted in the military:

> I was placed in a mental institution when I was 16. I dropped out of school when I was 16. I ran away and joined the U.S. Navy when I was 17, being 17 years in age and 6 feet, 6 inches, but with an emotional maturity of 10 years. The Navy is a frightening place.

A man who needed to get away from his alcoholic father said, "The best thing that happened was that I joined the Army."

The Long Process

Some participants reflected on the long, long process of getting away from the abuse. Moving out of the home was one step in this process. Moving away to another city or another state was another way to get away. Others talked about being in contact with their abuser, but not allowing the abuse to continue:

> The first right step I took was when I moved away at 20 to the city. . . . I never went back home alone again. I always go with my husband. I don't even open myself up for their verbal abuse and accusations, like I'm not doing a good job with the kids. . . . They only see me on my turf.

*   *   *

I have a business relationship with my abuser. I am currently attempting to sell the business and intend to move 200 miles away. I am running away from my abuser. I am running away from painful memories and control. I am running toward freedom.

Some participants described having no contact with the person who abused them or other family members who did nothing:

I graduated from high school so I could go away to school. Later I went into the Army to get even farther away. . . . One year into counseling I knew I had to tell my mother to get out of my life. Since then I have felt like I've been let out of prison.

*   *   *

I no longer have any relationship with my parents or my brother, for they continue to abuse me. I am not strong enough to protect myself from them.

*   *   *

I learned to understand and express how I felt. I also clung to the idea that somehow I could get my parents to become healthier, too. (I chuckle at this now.) At any rate, when I told him that he had hurt my feelings, he exploded, "Fuck you". . . . I can no longer be proud of these people. I don't like them, I don't like the way they treat me, and I don't like the way they make me feel. I severed all contact. My parents have made no attempt to reach me.

One woman said her parents died when she was seventeen and their death helped her transcend.

Although many severed ties with the family members who abused them, some reconnected after a time of therapy or processing the abuse. Sometimes there was a confrontation with the abuser; sometimes there was a reuniting with siblings. As one woman said about her relationship with a sibling, "There were years of alienation, and now we are very close as we have faced our past and shared it with each other."

LOOKING FORWARD, NOT BACK

A minority of people (24 percent) in the study said that looking forward to positive things, rather than dwelling on the past, was one of the things that helped them transcend a traumatic childhood. Many of these participants who talked about looking forward, not back were well on their way to transcending—they were likely to have examined what had happened to them, begun to heal, and wanted to move on. They had a positive attitude toward life and viewed the future with a sense of hope.

One person reflected on both the past and the present:

> I like talking about solutions, not the problems. I'm just doing today and have no energy or time to do what's past. . . . Life is too short to dwell on the past. I only have today.

> At some point we need to make the decision to simply grow up, no matter what has gone before and make the best we can of the rest of our lives—loving where we can, enjoying and having fun where we can, and leave the parts that are hard. We need to know it is—the same for all. Grasp the comfort of ceasing to see yourself as so different and share the joy of joining the human race.

Others added thoughts about the future:

> I accepted [at] around 9 or 10 years of age that things were not as I would like them to be, but that things would get better. I learned to live in the future. I continue to live in the future. . . . Although I can honestly say that I am pretty much content and happy with my life now, it is largely due to the fact that I have learned to accept that my behavior, attitudes, etc., and reflect on the damage caused by the circumstances of my childhood. It is largely due to the fact that I have programmed in a lot of positive behaviors and attitudes that serve me well.

> *   *   *

> I was able to separate the past, present, and future and deal with each separately. . . . They [my foster parents] believed that you could be the sum of your own choice and not the product of your past.

Some described their views about life as being positive, not negative. Is this a basic personality characteristic or is the development of a positive attitude something that happens gradually, along with transcending? We do not know.

> Life is worth living regardless of the trauma experience. You can look at it negatively or positively. I choose to look at it positively.

*   *   *

> I feel if I did not keep my positive attitude throughout my life, my life would have been 100 times worse than it has turned out.

Others talked about how it was not helpful to blame everything on what had happened to them in their past. The advice they gave was to move on, let go of the past, not to use it as an excuse for failure. One woman said, "I am living for today and not letting my past experiences dictate who I am or what I do." At one point in her life, another woman concluded, "Hey, your life is half over. When are you going to move on?" A man described it this way:

> There comes a time when you realize it's easier to let go and get on with life, rather than to harbor bad thoughts from the past. . . . I have tried to turn loose the ghosts of the past.

Another man had this to say:

> I always believe that life is what you make it. If you want a better life you will figure out a way to improve it, one way or another. If you didn't change it, you didn't want change bad enough.

One man described how the trauma in his life and the years of healing had made him realize that he was in a better place. Looking forward would now be easier:

> Because I have fallen to the pits of life and have clawed my way up to where I am now, I have a certain perspective which says

the lows I face will never be as low as they once were. And the highs will soar beyond imaginable previous highs.

Another woman said, "I'm not going to waste a good life being bitter about my childhood. . . . I'm a tough old broad."

One woman who lived through the war in Nazi Germany had this final advice about the past, present, and the future:

> Don't give up. Look forward, not back. Let go of the past, but do not forget the good or the bad.
>
> What was—was, it cannot be changed.
>
> What is—is, but it can be changed.
>
> What comes—comes, be on the offensive.

CONCLUSION

With age comes experience and sometimes wisdom and, as these children became adults, they developed independence and personal power. With growth came flashbacks. Nightmares and horrifying memories sometimes flooded their days. Things often got worse before they got better. But step-by-step, day-by-day, the movement tended to be forward as they continued along the journey of healing. One woman summarizes her recovery this way:

> My childhood experiences affected every aspect of my life including career choices and partner choices. My recovery, likewise, affected every aspect of my life. My recovery process is a lifetime commitment that leads me to places I never dreamed of. Giving up the image of the "ideal" family is shattering. I rocked many boats which are mired in thick muck.
>
> My recovery process has been most challenging. I lacked support. I found little support from professionals in the mental health field. I've faced life-threatening situations. I often felt alone, confused, overwhelmed. I could barely function for long periods of time. But once I opened the door to reality, to awareness, I knew I could never turn back. Turning back meant certain death. Going forward is full of uncertainties, but I feel alive.

I feel pain, anger, guilt, loneliness, shame, fear, and joy. But the joy and peace increase as I progress.

I do not know where I am going, but everything I've experienced has taught me that I am becoming well. I may not be rich or famous, but I am a success. I've given my children the greatest gift—recovery.

Transcending can also be defined as *going beyond* or *excelling*. As adults, these participants did go beyond and they did excel. Is it possible to ever go completely beyond the pain? Would it really be wise to do so? And, even though there is palpable fear for many that they will fail in their quest, there is a conscious, courageous effort to break the cycle of trauma and abuse.

What does it take as an adult to transcend a traumatic childhood? It can be best summed up in the words of a woman who said:

It is a combination of inborn personality, relationships I have in childhood, my faith in God, and a willingness as an adult to work hard in spite of the pain of remembering and healing.

We believe there is also evidence of the unrelenting human spirit.

Chapter 4

School

School is a place where young people spend almost as much time as they spend at home, and many of the participants talked about the role school played in their lives. For some it was a place of escape and refuge, a place to get away from what was happening at home. For others it was the place that contributed to the abuse or where the major form of abuse took place.

The four stories in this chapter describe in varying degrees how school helped these children survive a traumatic childhood, or how school made it worse. The first story is about a participant who was overweight and how the teachers did not protect her from the physical and psychological abuse she received from the other students. In addition, a school psychologist told her that it was a sin to overeat which made her conclude that she would go to hell.

The second story describes how a child was misdiagnosed in school as being retarded. She spent most of her high school years trying to prove to teachers and administrators that she did not belong in special education. She was also abused and teased by other students, and no one stopped it. In spite of everything, she made the honor roll in her senior year in high school and went on to college.

The third story includes a brief description of how school was a positive thing in a child's life. School allowed her to excel and be recognized based on her own achievements. It allowed her to mentally and physically escape from a family that was abusing her.

The fourth story describes a child who loved to read, to escape the reality of abusive parents. He did not find school a supportive or challenging place, with the exception of one teacher who saw his strengths.

Surviving and Transcending a Traumatic Childhood
© 2007 by The Haworth Press, Inc. All rights reserved.
doi:10.1300/5839_04

IT WAS A SIN TO OVEREAT

Emotionally and physically abused by her mother and teased mercilessly by her peers, this thirty-two-year-old European American woman describes herself as being overweight most of her life. Now, she suffers from a rare disease, but hopes someday to become an RN. This is her story:

I have always wanted to be famous, but not this way. I have been overweight most of my life. My mother made a big deal over food. I became a compulsive overeater. I believe I was physically and emotionally abused by my mother, and I think she was physically and emotionally abused by her mother, but she is in denial about this. I was told about a time I didn't want my mom to leave for somewhere, and she beat the hell out of me. My mom and dad couldn't communicate; he would tell me everything. But he did nothing to help me, although he always kept a positive attitude. She would win arguments by yelling and screaming. I learned to find comfort by eating.

School was not a good experience for me. I was not a good student and I was teased all the time. In the second grade I had lost weight and was down to a normal size, but in third-grade I got a teacher who just passed me on to get rid of me, as I was not a real smart student. My mother would always tell me that I was retarded when she was mad at me. When I asked her if that was true, she just wouldn't say anything about it, or would say something like she didn't like what I was wearing that day. I had no one to talk to except my mother, and when I talked to her she would use it against me when she was mad at me later. Because of my emotional state I gained all my weight back.

In seventh grade I can remember the day the math teacher was late to class. Because we were unsupervised, the other students tried to literally pop me with pencils. In ninth grade I had a science partner that tried to melt the fat off of me with a Bunsen burner. I had no hair on my arms because of this, but it took me seven months to convince the teacher that this was happening to me. Finally, it was decided that I should see a counselor, the school psychologist. He was the one that told me that it was a sin to overeat and be a glutton. I interpreted that to mean that I was going to go to hell for being fat.

I continued to gain weight and be teased in school until I was a senior and weighed close to 350 pounds. I never had a date. I was hardly ever asked to any social gatherings. I was very withdrawn, but I put up a good front to everyone. I didn't let anybody know that there was anything wrong. I thought of killing myself because it would stop the hurt of the teasing and the abuse. But I didn't do it because I was afraid I might become a vegetable and not be able to work and take care of myself. I used to burn myself with hot water though.

I think schools should teach their students that everyone is human. They should also try and stop the teasing that goes on. Maybe sending those kids to the principal's office or expelling them from school. For sure they should make them apologize to the one they teased. And they should be the ones to see the school psychologist. I believe that children who get teased have low self-esteem, and that possibly they are being abused or neglected at home. Also, if a child is grossly overweight as I was, the parents should be turned in to social services. They should be made to go for counseling, and be made to take some parenting classes, as there is obviously something wrong going on there.

I wish my mom could have gotten help. She made me go to groups called TOPS and Weight Watchers when I was young. I felt like a freak because I was the youngest one there. I attended 24 meetings, but I was made to go. It was not my fault that I was fat, but my mother told me it was. I had to put up with a lot from my mother. I just wanted to feel loved. One group that did help me when I was young was 4-H. They treated me like a human being. They didn't tease me, and I got a sense of accomplishment from belonging to it. Other than that there were no support groups for me in my area when I was young.

When I was 21 the farm crisis hit. My dad was very depressed. I wanted him to get help, but he got help for me instead. I saw a psychiatrist and someone finally believed in me. She told me I was worth something and could do something with my life. She made me see that I was being emotionally abused at home by my mother. She helped me to get out of my home and to make some friends. She helped me to get through LPN school and to get a job. I became an A and B student for the first time. I was a D and F student in high school. I also had the surgery where they staple your stomach.

I was raised a Catholic, but refused to go [to church] for a long time as I felt that God was not doing anything for me. I guess that's why dad stayed with mom. They got married in the Catholic church and he must have felt that he would lose the farm if they got a divorce. Now I think of myself as Catholic and go to church to help me deal with my past and present hurts.

I have never had a close relationship with anyone because I am afraid of getting hurt. I would like to marry, but I am afraid. I don't have a sex life because I fear sex and am so withdrawn. My mom and dad never shut the door to their bedroom when they were having sex when I was growing up. I could hear my mother making gross comments, like she didn't see how anybody would let anybody stick that gross thing in them. I want to be a parent and was planning on adoption, but now with my illness my plans have been put on hold.

As a child I felt different and as an adult I feel different from everyone else. I have always cried easily, it's no big deal. I was taught to accept everything that was handed to me. I became a nurse because I wanted to be a caretaker who tries to fix everything. But I've heard that a nurse is psychologically known as an angry caretaker.

Today I feel like my childhood has affected me both positively and negatively. I have learned that I am self-sufficient, trustworthy, unconditional, determined, loving, accepting, and willing to help anybody. Nothing can get me down. I am also just glad that I had the strength to live through it, but I am not trusting of others and I feel unloved. And now I have arthritis because of my obesity. I am bothered by my past, mostly at Christmas, in the spring, and at weddings, but I have become more comfortable talking about it in the last six years. I have had good dreams where I was skinny. And I have had nightmares where my ninth grade psychologist's house was burning and he could not get out because the windows were boarded up. I waved to him in my dream. Maybe this dream comes from the two fires that we had at home when I was six years old and when I was in the seventh grade. Another nightmare I've had is where I'm beating my mother with a vacuum cleaner hose.

Today it still hurts that I feel unloved and that I haven't had a steady relationship. I have learned that there are few people who like me, because not all parents abuse and not all kids tease. I have resolved my feelings about my past teasing, but my mother still makes me crazy, so I am working on that. It is a little easier though when I am not living with her, but now I am forced to because of my rare disease. I am unable to work but am presently working on becoming an RN.

I know that I have survived and transcended my childhood, because if I had only survived I would not have plans for the future. Hopefully, I will get my RN degree and maybe adopt, and hopefully be in a relationship someday and get on with my life. In the meantime I like to ski, do cross stitch, make pottery, bike, and play with my nieces. I also have had my number on a hot line to become a companion to a child who needs to talk.

Today I work hard to not let the abuse I suffered continue in my family. I now know that I can forgive those who hurt me in the past because they didn't know any better. But I'll never forget. I can only work on acceptance.

MY NICKNAME WAS "THE RETARD"

This forty-year-old European American woman was labeled as "retarded" in elementary school. She suffered through physical and emotional abuse. In high school she challenged the school system and eventually completed a two-year college degree, graduating with honors:

I was a child who had difficulty in school and got very poor grades. I remember having the most difficulty in reading. To make matters worse, our first-grade teacher was new and divided our class into three groups. I was in the bottom group and she rarely had time for us. We all fell behind. As we moved up in grades this lower group became smaller as students moved away. I became one of the few who had to leave the room to attend special classes. This caused the kids in my school to pick on me. I was called "The Retard."

After the name-calling had begun, financial hardship set in for my family. My father was a farmer and lost his dairy herd through disease. We had no income. My father became cold and uncaring. We were told regularly by him that we were no good. We often heard him say he was going to just leave us all to fend for ourselves. He never did, but it made an impression.

Because of our financial problems, I did not have many clothes. It was especially bad in about the sixth grade. It was embarrassing and the abuse at school got worse. In sixth grade I was at the third-grade level. I was sent on to junior high but the other remaining kids who went to a special class had either graduated out of it or were sent to a special school for the retarded.

I remember one girl ended up going to the school for the retarded. She was a friend of mine. I also felt she was smarter than me. She improved her grades and felt sure that she would avoid the school, but it did not work. I remained where I was and she went to the special school. I will never forget seeing her. When she went to the special school she changed. She just sat or stood and stared off into space. You could not even talk or play with her anymore. I don't know how she turned out, but she did not belong there. I only hope that after a year in this special school her family moved away and that she got on the right track again. This made me very afraid of the school and I made up my mind they weren't going to do this to me.

About the time I went on to junior high our school also consolidated with another school. I was really looking forward to it, because I thought I would be able to make friends with new blood in the school. Wrong! It got even worse. They would push me down into water holes, knock me down through flights of stairs, destroy my meals in the lunch room, kick me, stab me with sharp pencils, shoot pins at me with rubber bands, and call me sexual names which indicated I was worthless. It was so bad I could no longer go to lunch, and there wasn't much food at home so I lost 50 pounds. No one noticed. Instead, I was chewed out by school officials when I asked for a refund for my lunch ticket so I could give the money to my dad.

When I went on to high school I made some new friends, finally. I still had plenty of problems with the boys in my grade being abusive, and I even had some girls who called me names and harassed me, but I kept it hidden. No one in my family knew what I was going through. They didn't need this on top of already-existing problems. I really had no one to talk to during that time. My parents were poor and had too many problems of their own. Teachers would not listen. Even when they heard it, teachers didn't stop the torment. I was very close to my grandparents, but I did not tell them because I feared they would also dislike me. Still, my grandparents were a positive influence in my life because I could be myself around them without fear. I could talk to them and laugh. My sisters and brothers were too young. There was no one at home.

Only God knew my real pain. I had a faith in God that somehow this would end. Many prayers were said in private. I think it was my pillar of strength. I believe God is always there to listen. What we wish is not necessarily what we get, but somehow or in some way we will later see what the reason was for what we went through.

When I felt like I was going crazy I would compensate for all the hatred by living in an imaginary world where I was intelligent and accepted for what I was. I thought about killing myself because of feelings of worthlessness. I was of no value to anyone.

As I look back on this time, I remember always wondering what I had done wrong to deserve the name-calling and beatings. Teachers could have done something, but they made matters worse (I found out 20 years later). They were more against me than I realized. They had me pegged as mentally deficient and any attempt on my part to prove otherwise wasn't acknowledged.

In high school I was not allowed to take the courses I wanted. I was assured that they were way above my level and I would never be able to pass them. I was then told to take certain courses because there were not enough students in them. I wasn't able to pass these courses either, but they put me in them just because they needed to fill a class.

Despite everything that I seemed to have going against me my grades improved some. But, it looked as if I would not graduate with such a low grade-point average. By accident, during the summer, my fears were confirmed when I found a letter addressed to my parents which said I would not graduate and it would be best if I was removed from school and sent elsewhere so that I "could learn something manual and usable when I was of age." I made up my mind at this point that the school was no longer going to tell me what to do. I was going to take the classes I wanted. Finally the counselor gave in, but he said he would pull me out of a class as soon as he saw I was failing. I began by making up credits from courses I had failed the year before. It began to look like I could possibly graduate.

I remember having a fight with an English teacher. She would always ask, "Why are you doing so well in my class? You even do better than some of the top students in the grade." I just told her that I loved literature and it just came easy. I had also done well in a business class I had taken, and enrolled in a second course from this same teacher. I felt I had really blossomed in his class. He acted and treated me as if I knew my stuff. In this second class, he told me I earned an A! I had finally done it. I was so happy. But when I received my report card I had a C+. I never could get an acceptable explanation for why it had been changed. I didn't think that much about it and went on to improve all of my grades. I made the honor roll.

After graduating from high school, I went on to college to get an Associate of Arts degree in business. My grade point was 3.38 at graduation. I also took some courses toward a BA degree, but never completed it. I worked ten years in an office and became a supervisor. I don't think I would have been able to do it if it had not been for that teacher who saw my potential. No one else did.

It was 20 years later when I, again, met my bookkeeping teacher. He now runs a meat locker close to my sister and her husband. He told me I should know what happened that day so long ago when I came to him asking why my grade had been changed from an A to a C+. He said I had earned an A, but someone in the administration office saw my grades and had the A changed. My teacher had asked why, and the administrator said I wasn't capable of doing any better. My teacher protested, and they had a special meeting with school officials and my teachers. He convinced them all that I did what I did by sheer effort and nothing else. After this I was no longer told I could not take specific courses. It was up to me. When I got on the honor roll, my teachers and the counselor all went out of their way to congratulate me.

I have not seen a professional counselor or attended support groups. I resolved my problems by graduating from high school and being on the honor roll, making a 3.38 grade-point average in college, and making friends at work.

Some of the effects are still a part of me. Sometimes I am nervous and insecure around people because I fear they will hate me. I don't fear physical harm, but rather verbal harm. I also have a fear that I will fail and that people will not believe me. One problem did not show up until after I was married. My husband and I and our four children live very near my in-laws and they are very critical and complaining people. They lie and gossip, and past feelings do come back when I am around them. To alleviate the pain I have to avoid them or think of something positive when they talk to me, or they get the best of me. I have not told my children about what happened to me. I don't want them to think less of me.

I also have flashbacks of the beatings and name-calling. They are usually triggered by similar situations, for example when someone makes me feel stupid. As I look back, I think I had more strength at that time than I seem to have now. I don't know how I kept going.

I am very afraid of meeting the classmates who made my life so miserable. It will be 23 years and I am still scared to death of going to a class reunion. I sometimes have nightmares and relive what happened in the past, of being yelled at, hit, and pushed. No one comes near me because I am so awful. Sometimes the dreams are positive. I dream I get along with the abusive person and that we become friends.

In spite of all the flashbacks and insecurities I still feel that I have survived and transcended. My past has made me a better person, a fighter. I go ahead with things, not waiting to be told that I can't do it. I am now a problem-solver for others. People come to me for emotional support and advice, and I just love it! I have learned how to listen and speak when needed. Many people tell me that they feel as if they have known me all their lives.

ONCE THERE WAS A SEEDLING IN THE FOREST

Despite early years of abandonment by her mother, alcohol and sexual abuse by her father, and a home life of neglect and violence, this forty-one-year-old African-American woman feels she has done more than just survive her childhood. Read her story to learn how she feels she has at long last transcended her traumatic childhood by putting her life and its events in perspective. Through understanding the negative aspects of her life and accepting them as a part of her life, she now knows that she does not have to let them rule her life, but it is a continuous struggle:

My father was a chronic alcoholic. My mother spent most of her time fighting with him and with my older brother and demanding inappropriate, all-consuming attention and allegiance from me. Until I was seven we—my mother, father, brother, and myself—lived with my maternal grandmother. Then my parents rented their own house. I remember absolutely nothing about the two years or so that we lived in that house. Other blocks of time are also erased from my memory. I am aware of my father molesting me when I was 14. I assume that he molested me before then as well, explaining, perhaps, my memory losses.

Our home was filled with tension, yelling, fighting, broken things. I remember being too embarrassed to have friends over. When I did, my father always appeared in the middle of my fun, drunk out of his mind. Holidays, vacations, birthdays were always a disaster: my father drunk; my mother angry, uncommunicative, and leaning on me for comfort. But, what could I do for her as a child?

My older brother and I never got along, in large part because my mother insisted that I take sides—hers—in the family. He and I fought often. To this day though we do talk to each other occasionally, it is always strained.

My mother had a habit of leaving the house whenever my father got drunk. Often, I would hear them fighting, then I would hear the car leaving the driveway. She would just take off and leave my brother and me with my father.

After we moved to Oregon in 1961, my parents adopted two children. So, at age 14 or 15, I became big sister to two infants. My older brother was out of the house by then. My mother's time was still taken up with dealing with my father. So, I eventually became my siblings' surrogate mother. (In African-American families, the oldest girl is often expected to take care of other family members and share, or bear, the responsibilities of the mother.) My sister even called me "Mommy" for a while. Still, when my parents would fight, my mother would take off. These times leaving me with a drunken father and two babies. I hated all of them, including my brothers and sister. It seemed as though I was the only sane person in a family of lunatics. Then I'd start to wonder about myself, particularly when I'd be depressed or think about killing myself.

I was generally a quiet child, one who keeps things in, only to have them come out in other ways. I had stomach aches, rashes, and nervous problems throughout my childhood. It seemed useless to turn to my family for help, so I didn't.

Besides my father molesting me, one of my older brother's friends and the husband of one of my mother's friends molested me when

I was approximately 11 and 15 years old, respectively. Neither my life nor my body seemed to be under my control.

Along with physical ailments, the situation in my family resulted in my sucking my thumb, causing severe malocclusion, and wetting the bed until I was 13. I also developed a stutter which I still have today. Sometimes I try to think about what was good during my growing up. There were a number of things. But even now, they are often overshadowed by what was unpleasant.

I think that I survived my childhood by emotionally cutting myself off from my family as much as I could and focusing on school. I always liked school and did well. School was a place where I had some control over my life. It got me away from home. I could have fun and excel. Also, no one knew my family. In the seventh grade, I went to a newly built school and entered a new program for gifted students. I made new friends. I felt proud of myself for I had the opportunity to excel based on my own achievements, and I had the opportunity to be known apart from my family. My parents valued education and learning, but they did not impart any particular religious or spiritual beliefs to me. They were both intelligent and hard working. But, even so, I feel that schools could do more to sensitize their teachers to children that are in need of help. More training in family violence, substance abuse, etc., and the impact of it all on children could really help. Schools need to understand that the quiet and academically competent students can be just as troubled as the students who act out and have problems getting high grades.

I also developed a "tough hide" and a *strong* sense of independence and self-sufficiency. My ability to entertain myself, to trust myself and no one else, my love of reading, my love of quiet and solitude, and my being able to be alone for periods of time all helped me to survive and transcend. Still, I always wished that my maternal grandmother could have helped me by taking me away. But she and my aunt never talked to me and never helped me even though they knew about my father. I guess they were afraid to intervene and, therefore, felt helpless. Our moving to Oregon and adopting my little brother and sister only made things worse. If only my mom would have gotten a divorce and taken us away, my life would have been much different.

After my father was killed in 1982, I went into an emotional tail-spin. I had moved to Ohio in 1978, again trying to separate myself from my family. I entered therapy in 1987 after cutting off contact from my mother. Her need to be emotionally dependent on me was literally driving me crazy. After five years of therapy and some time on antidepressants, I emerged a much happier, self-confident, and calm woman. I have just recently reestablished contact with my mother after seven years. Not talking to her, in my opinion, was the key to my getting well.

I knew all along that my family was different and sick. Sometimes, when I was young my mother would talk about it, but I knew before then. About seven or eight years ago as a starting point in my recovery, I attended an Adult Children of Alcoholics (ACOA) meeting briefly. I felt I had to do something or I would die. I liked hearing stories like mine. I disliked the fact that everyone was white. I attended eight meetings but felt this self-help group was ineffective for me. I was seriously depressed and eating compulsively. I was having dreams about committing suicide. That was when I entered therapy and cut off contact from my mother. It saved my life.

Reliving things in therapy was very overwhelming. But, wanting to go to sleep and never wake up, feeling helpless, hopeless and un-worthy, depressed, lacking control, and fearing that the pain would never end made me stick with it for five years. I wanted to find out what my life would be like on the other side of the pain. I also needed someone to talk to as I was always choosing emotionally unavailable partners. I usually worked full time and went to school, at least part time, to keep myself busy and unavailable to others because I couldn't trust anyone. I was argumentative and I really feared intimacy.

I have never wanted to be married. I have always wanted to be able to get out of a relationship easily if I needed to. Being molested led to my hating my body, making sexual contact uncomfortable. The com-bination of that and an attempted rape at the age of 25 led to my de-veloping vaginal anesthesia, which I still have.

The vicious cycle that some families get into of passing on their pain and problems will not happen with me. I have already seen it happen in my family with my grandparents, my parents, myself, and my older brother and his family. I have never wanted to have children.

So there is not a chance that I will pass it on to my descendants because I won't have any.

Today, I have limited and rather strained contact with my three siblings. While I still have some problems trusting others, in the last five years I have had a number of close, satisfying relationships with same-gender partners and friends. As to the sexual aspect of my life, I feel like a vital part of my life has been robbed. I can talk about it with my partner, but I may return to my therapist to see if I can work this out further. After telling my story so many times in therapy and discovering that I did not die after talking about it, it is much easier to discuss it now. I know, too, that bad events don't mean the end of your life. Choices still exist.

As I look back at my life now, I can see not only the negative but also the positive sides of it. On the negative side there is a loss of family and lots of fears. I fear intimacy; sexual contact; people who drink alcohol; crowded, noisy places or places where people drink; failure; not being perfect; disclosing too much; being angry and depressed all of the time; having to spend lots of time and money on therapy; and unsuccessful relationships. Also, I still think daily about my troubling times and certain holidays, such as Christmas, are especially hard. But, even though I still think about everything, these thoughts don't trouble me so much anymore. Sometimes old behaviors and fears pop up, but much less frequently. I've also had hundreds of flashbacks about what happened to me. The most common one is like a series of still pictures in my mind that replay my father molesting me at age 14. Even though it seems like the pictures are still always there, they don't disturb me as much now. So I know I'm getting better.

On the positive side these are the things that therapy has helped me learn about myself: I'm intelligent, articulate, creative, organized, empathetic, a good friend, a hard worker; I can endure difficulties to get what I want; I am comfortable being alone if I need to be; I'm independent; I have the ability to "read" people; I know how to protect myself; I am fulfilling my plans and goals; I am in a healthy relationship now; I can laugh and have fun. I am also learning how to forgive, as I think I prefer it to holding grudges. Therefore, I am working on reconnecting with my mother. I believe I have a moderate and growing level of self-esteem. I like myself.

Career-wise, my experiences have undoubtedly influenced my professional life. I am a certified chemical dependency counselor and trainer. I do training, program development and facilitation, and I have a home-based counseling and referral program. I work with a lot of drug-using parents who are trying to stay clean and take better care of their children. I have worked with many clients with similar backgrounds to mine. I am an excellent listener.

My advice to others who would like to help a child or an adult who is going through, or has been through, a traumatic childhood would be to listen and do not give advice. Also, don't assume anything. Don't act based on the parents' discussion of the situation. If at all possible, ask the child directly.

In the future I will continue my counseling and training work. I look forward to personal happiness and professional success. Peace of mind and trusted friends.

Lastly, here is a story I wrote that best illustrates how my childhood experiences affected my life overall:

> Once there was a seedling in the forest. It was overshadowed and crowded by all the big trees. Every year rain, wind, snow, animals and the boots of hikers would batter the seedling. Surely, its newly-sprouted leaves would wither, die and fall off. But, amazingly, some people came along and cut down the trees that crowded the seedling the most, giving it room to feel the sun and grow faster and healthier. The seedling liked being able to see and feel the sun. Years later, the seedling turned into a tall, beautiful tree that never crowded other trees in the forest.

LIFE IS WHAT YOU MAKE IT

Growing up in an alcoholic, violent family, this thirty-two-year-old European American man describes himself in childhood as having a very bad temper and low, low self-esteem. Now as an adult after surviving two marriages, one divorce, and a brain injury in a motorcycle accident, he feels he is happily married having learned from his mistakes. He believes his story could fill 100 pages with painful childhood memories:

I grew up in a house with an alcoholic father. He was also a work-aholic and emotionally and physically the strongest individual I've ever seen in my life. My mother and he fought very often. I had three younger brothers. Father never touched us kids when he was drunk but he did hit my mother occasionally. When I was ten, my five-year-old brother burned down half of our house. This brother was seriously burned in that fire from head to toe. That incident happened in 1970 and it made a profound mark on all of us.

In 1973 this same brother was seriously burned again when he was playing with gasoline. At that time a cousin kicked a jar filled with gas into a fire and it went all over my brother's legs.

For a good five or six years my parents fought constantly. It seemed like they fought even more because of the fires. Both of them had affairs and they separated five or six times before divorcing after 18 years of marriage. Their divorce made everything worse for us. We had to sell our house and then we had to move around a lot into rented houses. My mother put herself in a mental institution a number of times through the years. She was hooked on legal drugs then, and still is.

Seeing my younger brother in pain, and listening to and watching my parents fight took its toll on me both physically and emotionally. Some trauma I realized right away. But other effects, like the trauma of my parents' fighting and my father drinking, took years for me to realize. I grew up with a very bad temper, especially as a teenager and into my late 20s, and I had low, low self-esteem. I fought with my mother a lot while I was growing up. I also was always in fights at school. I was always pretty much of a daredevil or thrill-seeker all my life.

I actually lived in a very "open" family. We were all very close and comfortable with one another. We could all talk to each other and none of us was afraid to ask personal questions. If father could have stopped drinking maybe my parents wouldn't have fought and things could have been different for us. Even though I could talk with both of my parents I feel that I basically raised myself pretty much. And most of what I learned I went after with no help from anyone. I always believed that life is what you make it. If you want a better life, you will figure out a way to improve it, one way or another. If you don't change it, you didn't want change bad enough.

My secret of getting through the tough times was a very active imagination and the love of reading. I would go off and wander or explore nearby woods. Or I would go to the library or my room and get lost in a book. My mother read a great deal to me and my brothers when we were young. I fell in love early with reading biographies, and books about history. I feel that I raised my self-esteem by reading about great people in history. I enjoyed reading about military greats such as Patton, Grant, Pershing, Alexander, and Rommel, and also about people such as Lincoln, F. Lee Bailey, and Kennedy. I also had a weakness for comic books.

Today, I still love to read and write. I think this has always been my way to escape reality. Unfortunately, I was bored with most of what they taught me in school and I quit in 11th grade. Some teachers gave me a positive view of life, but very few of them did. My sixth-grade teacher was the first teacher I had that stuck up for me and saw my strengths in school. I fought a lot but I didn't start the fights. I just didn't walk away from them. This sixth-grade teacher saw that and stuck up for me many times. I've always felt that most of what they teach in school is a waste of time. I don't feel that they teach the important things.

If I could give teachers some advice I'd tell them to look at each child as an individual. To listen to them and ask them how you can help. Talking is the best remedy. Looking at children and talking to them only in a teaching mode tells you nothing about that child. Each child is like a snowflake, no two are alike. Teachers have to realize that they, too, can still learn by really listening to each child.

I was brought up and baptized a Protestant. When I was 16 to 17 years old I told everyone that I was an atheist; that I didn't believe in God. My religious beliefs have changed several times over the years. Now that I'm older and have gone through so much—I was shot at in the jungles of Central America while in the Army, I've been in two serious motorcycle accidents, I've experienced the birth of my daughter, and many other incidents—I've changed my beliefs. I believe in God now.

I got my GED right away after I quit school because I fell in love and got married. Even though I always felt loved by my parents I think that their divorce was the most tragic event in my life. I wanted someone who would always be there and who I knew loved me. But my marriage was a disaster, however, for about seven out of the ten years it lasted. It was filled with violence because of my temper. I was always fighting with my wife over stupid things—problems that were my fault, but I blamed them on her instead. I don't think I respected my female companions the way I should have.

At 23, I went into the Army. It was the best thing that happened to me. It helped me get ahead in countless ways. I got to travel all over the world, and that in itself was an education that you can't put a price on. Next, I got divorced, and remarried again at 28.

While I was in the Army and stationed in Minnesota, I was involved in a serious motorcycle accident. I received a laceration to the left front of my brain causing my emotions to be severely heightened. I went to a support group after my brain injury in 1988. For at least three to three-and-a-half years I was struggling with my emotions. I was then retired from the Army. After a year or so I went to college with VA vocational rehabilitation help, and graduated with an Associate of Arts degree in law enforcement and criminal justice in July of 1992.

I think the biggest influence all the violence in my childhood had on me was the effect it had on my patience and temper. Both were short all my life until the last few years. I had many emotional problems as a child, then when I was involved in that motorcycle accident when I was 28 my brain injury heightened my emotions to an unbelievable level. But it finally enabled me to be able to talk with others about my past. At the present time I still have emotional problems, but they are more positive now. It seems to have opened up my mind more. I am more aware of others' feelings. The only drawback to it all is that my feelings get hurt easier, and I feel other people's tragedies so much more. Overall, I feel that I am a much more balanced person because of all of these events in my life.

Other effects of my childhood are the many flashbacks I've had. I've had so many that there are too many to write down. Things like having a hard time with money, arguments with my wife, or yelling at my daughter bring them on. I also know that I haven't resolved everything from my past. Different memories come back to me when I'm experiencing emotional pressure. I now see things in various ways due to my upbringing. I've also felt personal guilt, and I've blamed others for my trauma as a child. There were also times when I felt that I was going "crazy" because of it, but I was never suicidal because of it. I hate pain and love life no matter how bad it is at times. Who knows what tomorrow brings?

When things get difficult for me now I think back, because it's hard to imagine that things would ever be as bad as when I was a kid. For unexplained reasons I cannot hold a grudge for very long. If my wife and I have a disagreement I forget about it much earlier than she does. But I am also able to get through all these things because I've stayed active in work, reading, and talking my problems out with whoever would listen. I've no fear in talking to people about it. Not that I do it too often, but if someone asks I do not have a problem with it. I might get emotional about it, but I will still talk about it. Most people who know me say that I would be a good counselor because I love to talk and motivate people. I'm a good listener, I'm told. I know how to look inside of everyone close to me, instead of looking at their exterior.

Because of my past I stay completely away from alcohol and drugs myself. I don't care for people who drink more than an occasional drink or two. I am a big defender of children's rights. When I see other people hurting, especially children, it really hurts me today. I am brought to tears at least once or twice a week, just from seeing others suffer on TV or reading about suffering in the newspaper. Before I had a child of my own I joined the "Big Brother" program where I lived. I was involved with two young boys who came from a violent and broken home. I still keep in touch with them to this day.

I am now happily married, having learned from my mistakes. I have one daughter and another child is on the way. Sometimes I have worried about repeating the vicious cycle I was in with my own children. Actually, I do fail at times, but on the positive side I always, always work to be a better husband and father. I am constantly looking for ways to be a better parent. I do not want my children to go through what I went through. I plan on devoting my life to my children in the hope that I can raise happy and emotionally-healthy kids.

Today I think that I have survived and transcended my childhood. I feel that if I had not kept my positive attitude throughout life, my life would have been 100 times worse than it has been. Other people also tell me I am okay today. I've always had something to "push" me to better myself. I always strive to not let my problems get the best of me. I have learned that life is unpredictable. But, when life gets bad I always tell everyone that something good must be coming. I know that if I set my mind to it, I can accomplish *anything* I want. I think the future will bring me good things.

Chapter 5

Religion and Spirituality

We have stated that religion and spirituality were part of the lives of participants in this study. The three people who tell their stories in this chapter provide examples of how their relationship with God helped them through their difficult times and how their religious and spiritual beliefs evolved over time.

Spirituality is discussed in the first story briefly, but poignantly, by a woman who received a message from God at the age eight that she could not kill herself because she needed to protect her little sister from her sexually abusive father. She began sleeping with the Bible under her pillow. Today she continues to take God's message about helping children seriously. She has a professional career helping parents protect their children from abusers.

The second story is one that we heard often from participants. Religious beliefs, as taught to these abused children by parents and church leader, portrayed God as punishing and hurtful. In adulthood, these beliefs about God were discarded, to be replaced with a belief in a loving and accepting God. This woman blames the God of her childhood for what happened to her and credits the God of her adulthood for helping her recover.

In the third story, a woman describes her belief in God as a child and how it helped her feel loved when her family thought she was unlovable. As an adult she found metaphysics, which provided a spiritual belief system that was critical to her healing.

Surviving and Transcending a Traumatic Childhood
© 2007 by The Haworth Press, Inc. All rights reserved.
doi:10.1300/5839_05

I WAS SEXUALLY ABUSED BY MY FATHER
AND MY MOTHER TRIED TO KILL ME!

This thirty-four-year-old, European American woman with two children lived with abuse from both her mother and her father for seventeen years. She then married a man who was abusive. She has survived and transcended the trauma in her life without the help of counseling or support groups:

My father began sexually molesting me at age three. He would have me suck on his penis. It progressed to anal penetration when I was eight. I told my mother and grandmother about it and they refused to believe it. As a result, at age three my grandmother "helped" me down the stairs in such a way that my collar bone was broken. When I was eight I asked for help again. This time I was thrown against a wall and received a fractured tailbone.

At that point I felt I had become an adult. I tried to hang myself with my mother's tape measure, but panicked when the tape measure broke, because I knew I'd be in trouble for breaking the tape measure. After I tried to hang myself with the tape measure I had a dream that God told me he still needed me to protect my little sister, who was born two years later, and to help other children. This gave me a purpose for living.

When I was eight years old I started sleeping with the Bible under my pillow. When I was 16 I was afraid my father had gotten me pregnant. This time when I asked my mother for help she threw a knife at me and it stuck in my arm. When the baby was due I was told to leave home and never come back. When I left I called a crisis line and was put on hold for five minutes. I decided, screw it, no one will help me but me. I did try suicide two more times. I slit my wrists at age 16 and swallowed tranquilizers at 20.

I had a baby sister who was born when I was ten. The bastard (my father) told me that I was always protecting her. When I left the farm I told my mother she better protect my sister. I also made her stop beating my little brother and sister by telling her if she was going to hit them she had to hit me first, and she better make it damn good because I was going to hit back. I told my father that I'd never bring up the past as long as he promised to leave my sister alone. I told him face-to-face that if I ever found out he messed with my sister I would come after his balls with a meat cleaver!

School was a negative experience except that it was a place to escape. I had no friends except my books and my teachers. I poured myself into schoolwork. Growing up I was allowed to bathe once a week in two inches of water, and was allowed to wash my hair once a month. It's no wonder I had no friends.

My mother would sometimes rip flesh off my arms with her finger nails, to get my attention. Sometimes when things got difficult I would dig my own "claws" into my arms. Even as an adult I sometimes discover that I am pinching my arms.

I felt so isolated. I was denied love and affection. To the outside world we were the perfect church-going family, but life at home was hell. The only person to turn to was God. He told me I was good, not a three-year-old slut, as my grandmother says. I once asked a school counselor for help and the SOB laughed at me. I also asked a pastor for help, and he said he couldn't get involved. I suppose my mother felt she would lose her means of support if she helped me. I suppose they were all afraid of going out on a limb alone to help, sort of like a rat that's afraid to jump from a sinking ship. My mother said that as a three-year-old I was seducing my father. My wish is that she would have loved me enough to protect me.

I went to college and graduated with a 3.98 grade-point average. I met a man who told my parents to "go to hell." I didn't love him but married him because I felt he "rescued" me from my past. Unfortunately, I went from the frying pan into the fire. While I was married I spent years looking down the barrel of a gun, being thrown across rooms, and being threatened. I finally had enough and felt my children's safety was at stake: one was 18 months and the other was three years. I packed the kids in the car and crossed the state line in the middle of the night. At that point I started from scratch.

The abuse stayed with me during my adult years through dreams. When I was married I could not let my husband touch me when I was asleep. I would scream, thinking dad had come for me. I haven't had many flashbacks since I've been on my own except when I had to "detail" my father's attacks for his counselor. I also would have dreams and would wake up in the middle of the night screaming. Generally, I was dreaming there was a naked man chasing me as a little girl. I would also have good dreams. I would dream that I had been left with a family that really loved me or that I was entirely by myself out in the country.

I began doing work with abused children for awhile and eventually was asked to work on the preventative end of things. I've worked with several programs which help parents learn how to protect their children. I am nationally known in this field. My goal is to drastically reduce the statistics for abused, kidnapped, and runaway children.

One of the things which has helped me is to look at a picture of me when I was three. I look at the picture and tell the little girl in that picture that she is a good and sweet and loving child. She did nothing wrong and I love her very much. I have never gone to counseling and I have never attended a support group. Not bad, huh? Each person is a unique individual and has to find their own way to heal.

Recently, I told my father to get help. I told him that I had aided in putting numerous offenders behind bars and felt guilty that he was an admitted pedophile running around free. I gave him 30 days to get actual help or I was going to turn him into the justice system, and I was going to monitor his progress. If he hadn't followed through I would have turned him in to authorities. I still fantasize about taking a meat cleaver to his balls and shoving them down his throat. (I'm really a nonviolent person.) Insisting my father get help and him admitting his responsibility for the abuse has been a positive step for me. I'm no longer intimidated by my father. I have taken the experience and tried to make it positive by protecting other children. Yes, I feel I have survived and transcended. One of the things which have been helpful in transcending is the opportunity to help protect other children through all the public speaking I have done.

So where is my family at today? My mom and dad have worked out their differences. My sister is a basket case. My little brother is a druggie. And my dad may still lose his balls!

Where am I today? I feel I have a lot for which to live. Although I have many wonderful friendships I have a hard time getting too close to a man. I'm very independent. I wanted children so bad, but was afraid I would do the wrong thing. I have two children, ten and eleven. I haven't done anything yet, and I don't think I will. My children know about my childhood. I've warned my children to never be alone with grandpa because he does things like "bad touch." They don't see their grandpa except at funerals and weddings. Their grandma got help and has told them about the abuse herself.

I am claustrophobic (hate small spaces). I used to be afraid of the dark and am extremely scared of electrical appliances or anything that vibrates. Physically I have developed ulcers and the inner lining of my anus was torn. I still have problems with my tail bone because it didn't heal properly.

What still hurts is that a trusting figure could betray an innocent child's trust. It hurts when I see others in pain because they've also been betrayed. I'll hold the child, pray for the child, and love the child. When a child has been sexually abused, the thing they need most is the thing they are most afraid of, and that's a hug.

I wrote a poem when I was ten years old which expressed my inner pain:

> Outside I am smiling
> Inside I am crying
> Yet no one can see.
>
> Outside I am laughing
> Inside I am screaming
> Yet no one can hear.
>
> Is there anyone
> Out there who
> Could see or hear?
> Is there anyone
> Out there
> Who could
> Understand?

Now as an adult I can see, I can hear, and I can understand.

As I said before, I had a dream when I was eight that God wasn't finished with me yet, and that I was supposed to help other children. The dream was right. God had plans for me. I only hope I can live up to his expectations.

INSIDE I WAS DYING

It has been five years since this European American woman's trauma ended. She is now twenty-five, works forty hours a week as a

dental assistant, and has asked for a divorce from her alcoholic hus-
band. She states that the stressful times in her life go as far back as
she can remember. A lot of it she can't remember, but she knows her
life was filled with emotional abuse, neglect, violence, mental illness,
physical illness, and sexual abuse. Today, with counseling and a
better understanding of her family's problems, she feels optimistic
about the future. She has faced up to her past and confronted her fam-
ily. More importantly, she has broken the silence in a way that her
family members have not yet dared to do:

I'm not sure where to start. I was born in California. We lived there
for five years. I don't remember a lot from then except the day we
moved. My parents told me we were going to the beach. We ended up
in North Dakota. This beach had snow. I was confused.

Sometime after moving up north I remember once sitting at the
dinner table getting ready to eat. My parents worked two different
shifts at this time, so only my dad was home with us. My sister was to
say grace, so she started out but my dad slapped her across the face.
He told her she was wrong and to do it over. She started again and he
slapped her again. This went on over and over, faster and faster, for
what seemed like a half an hour. I remember sitting there across from
her, I'm about six or seven at the time, and feeling paralyzed. I kept
praying to myself, "Get it right, get it right." The problem was that
she *was* doing it right; it was just the way we learned in Sunday
school. I wanted to help her but I was so small.

We talked about this incident again about a year ago. She told me
that all the food was on the table and that our brother was on the other
side of the table. I don't remember anything else though, as I was focused only on her face. She had long blond hair at that time and it kept
flying back and forth when he hit her across the face. Then it would
stick to the tears on her face. I remember how red her face was. Apparently my brother told him to stop, but dad said to sit down or else.
My sister was quick to point out when we talked of this that he had
stood up for her. I think that's why my sister doesn't like me a lot.
I think she wanted me to do something. But what could I do? Whenever we brought this up to dad later, he said that he couldn't remember anything. But all three of us kids do.

After this incident mom and dad started working the same night
shift together. My mom was around when my father was with us, but

she wasn't around when I needed her at night. She always said not to say or do anything to make dad angry and not to talk to anyone about our private lives. It's like she didn't care what went on as long as we looked good to the rest of the world. She told me recently that she had been extremely frightened that my dad would leave us. I think her reasoning was that she was trying to keep our family together at all costs, because she was an orphan. Her mom had left her when she was only 5 years old, and then her dad died when she was 12. My question is: What did it cost us?

I never told anyone about my life. I couldn't talk to anyone. My whole life was one secret after another. It was always a lot of lies. I wish my mom, brother, or sister could have helped me. They could have told me the truth. Then I would have known that my dad was crazy and not me. But, instead, I felt responsible for *everything* that happened. I felt like there was something wrong with me. I felt guilty for *living* because no one else saw reality in my family like I did.

I stayed away from home a lot. There was school, church, tap lessons, and Girl Scouts. Being around people who saw things the same way I did made me not feel crazy. School was safe. You used your intellect, not your emotions. I was good in school, I received good grades. I felt more normal there, but I had problems with friendships growing up. I wanted to be popular, to be "normal." I idolized a friend of mine for four years in grade school.

I think that school counselors need to be more in touch with children. The school system seems to think that if you're a straight-A student and don't cause trouble, you're healthy and everything is okay. You kind of fall through the cracks and counselors don't bother you. The thing they didn't know is that I was a wonderful actress and an expert in not causing trouble. Inside, I was dying.

We went to church every Sunday. I think having faith in God—I'm a Catholic—helped me through a lot of rough times. But as a child I used to be really afraid of God, because of everything my father taught me. My dad used to read to me all the time about the end of the world as written in the Bible. I was scared. Now my faith is strengthened. My God is not the same as my father's. I always know that there is a place I can go and be fully accepted. Even though my priest was no help when my husband and I were having problems in our marriage, I know that God will always love and forgive me.

When I was growing up I kept saying over and over to myself, "You'll get through this, it won't matter. You'll still get married and have children." I wanted to get married and have a "normal" life. Getting married was going to fix everything, and my husband would make me happy. (Okay you can get off the floor and stop laughing now.) That was very important to me. You can imagine how hard it was to see that my marriage was screwed up, and for me to ask for a divorce. For a long time I had sex and love fused together. I wanted to have sex a lot, and when I got denied I was hurt and thought my husband didn't love me. I finally have that all straightened out.

My husband, however, drank a lot. He kept promising me over and over that he'd quit drinking, but he didn't. Then he committed adultery. I asked for a divorce after that, and put myself into codependency treatment. (I had heard about this treatment through a godsend of a friend of mine.) After I decided to go into treatment, my husband decided to go into treatment, too. In treatment my denial system was broken down. I had several realizations: first that my husband was an alcoholic, and secondly that I had been sexually abused as a child. When I started treatment they asked me what my family was like when I was growing up. I told them that it was *perfect*. In reality I knew that it wasn't perfect so it was at this time that I also began looking into my dad's so-called nerve pills. He is supposed to be taking the drug, Stelazine, and one of its uses is for nonpsychotic anxiety attacks. It sounds like he has something more than just a nervous disorder.

It then became clear that I needed more intensive individual therapy, and because of things that came out during these sessions I decided to confront my whole family with my findings. My therapist and I called in my family for a group therapy session. Only my sister didn't show up. She is also married to an alcoholic, but I believe he beats her. I told them about the abuse that I now remembered that went on when I was growing up. They minimized it or denied it. I didn't care. I had done what I wanted to do, which was talk about it.

The next day after our meeting I found out the truth about my dad. He wouldn't talk to me about it during the session. He said that he had something else to tell me at home. You see, he believed that he couldn't talk at the session because the FBI might find out. Is the picture getting clearer? He then told me a long, bizarre story about how these people were trying to kill him etc., etc. So that's why we'd moved to Indiana so long ago, to get away from them. But he still doesn't feel safe, because they followed us here from Pennsylvania. He sees them on the freeway pushing some button in their cars when he goes past them.

Now I understand my father much better, since I finally know for a fact that he is mentally ill. I used to be scared of him. It still hurts that mom lied to me about dad's illness, but now I know that she lied because she thought that it was the only way for her to make each of us happy. Still, it made me not trust her. Also, I know she did it to keep us together because of her own childhood fears of abandonment. If we'd stayed in Pennsylvania maybe dad would have gotten help, but I think mom was afraid that they would probably have locked him up, tearing the family apart, which she feared above all else. Now my mom and I talk about *everything,* at my prompting of course, and I can tell her how I feel about things.

During the family session it really hurt me that my brother said he couldn't remember sexually abusing me, so I don't know what to do next about him. We have a very surface relationship. And, as my sister didn't even show up, I know it'll be very hard to ever get close to her also. I just remember how the three of us used to fight like hell when we were young. Maybe things will never change or get better for us. At least now I know that there is a reason for everything. And that the answer will become clear when it's time. I really believe that everything turns out for the best, even if it's not what you want. I now know that I am here for a reason. I am not crazy. I count. I am lovable.

My past has made me more compassionate toward other people with similar or different problems, because I know what it feels like to be different. I felt different from others as a child, and now, as an adult, I still feel different. But after I confronted my family it became easier for me to talk about my past. The more people I've told, the easier it has gotten to talk about it, although I'm not comfortable talking about it with just anyone, it depends on who I'm talking to. I do listen to my friends and let them know my story. I talk to my friend's children, and let them know that if they can't go to mom or dad, they can come to me. I think you should let children know that it's okay to talk about their problems, and assure them that they are safe. They need to know that they are "okay" as people. It's very important to let them know that it's not their fault and that they are not to blame. I know this because I used to blame myself for my problems. I also blamed my mom, my dad, my husband, and then God. I liked to hold resentments. They gave me a false sense of power. Finally, I have learned to not hold these resentments against anyone any more. I have learned the power of forgiveness. Most importantly, I learned to forgive myself. I can't forgive anyone else if I don't forgive myself first. I now believe that the only person you hurt by not forgiving is yourself. It's very liberating to know this.

With adults I'd stress listening. I'd also talk to them about their stressful times. Ask them what you can do to help. Ask them how things are going from time to time. Offer to go with them to therapy, support groups, meetings, etc. Suggest they read books on the subject. Tell them to have patience as it takes a *long* time to recover.

I guess I'd say that I have to give credit to lots of people and things for helping me to recover. There were friends, the codependency treatment, even TV Shows such as *Oprah* were helpful to me, books, Al-Anon, my husband, God, women's support groups, therapy, and even myself. I received a lot of support and love from the ladies I have been in support groups with. It was very hard for me to go to my first group meetings, because I was ashamed, I didn't want to talk to a group, and I didn't trust others easily. But after going to private therapy for awhile I finally tried a group and I liked it. Some can be expensive though. But I like the way people listen to you when you talk, and how they are interested in what you have to say. I like feedback. Sometimes we wouldn't have enough time. I've probably been to about 200 support group meetings, and if I knew exactly what illness my father has I'd go to a support group for learning how to deal with that. Whatever happens I know I'll continue in groups and in being open about my problems with others, because these things have helped me and have helped others in their journey toward recovery. Who knows what else I'll do to help in the future.

Today, I'm much better educated on a variety of family problems than my ancestors. But even though I have broken the *silence* on what was passed down to me, it still scares the hell out of me to become what I want very badly to be, and that is a parent. I'm afraid I won't be good enough. I'm also afraid that my father's condition will afflict one of my children. I know that nothing could make me repeat the cycle with my own children when I have them, but it's still very painful for me today to know that I hurt a boy a long time ago. You see, when I was eleven years old I molested a young boy. So far I have chosen not to find him and make amends at this point. Indirectly I feel I am helping children by giving to children's charities, causes, etc. Maybe your questionnaire should have asked the question, "Have you ever treated someone else the way you were treated?"

As an adult I have different strengths and weaknesses that normally I wouldn't have had if I hadn't gone through what I did as a child. On the positive side I can see both sides to any issue, and I have a great sense of humor that I developed a long time ago in order to survive. I'm also kind, loving, courageous, careful, and responsible. I like to lift weights because it makes me feel strong and in control of my body. Presently, I am in a service job taking care of people's needs. I do enjoy it, though I didn't go on to college after high school because it would have upset our family balance.

On the negative side I don't trust easily, I'm suspicious, emotional, controlling, and judgmental. I'm also very jumpy and anxious. I'm scared of anything under my bed. I think maybe someone hid there once. But my biggest fear is not being good enough. I'm still working on my ability to interact positively with other people, and I'm trying to build my self-esteem. Being in Girl Scouts and taking tap lessons when I was a child helped some with this quality.

I also have a very sensitive stomach and I get really bad colds, probably because of my emotional state which causes my immune system to run down sometimes. I used to think daily about my bad times, but now as I work through it it's less and less, maybe just weekly. I do have flashbacks, about 50 so far, that are more often through my sense of smell than visual. I think it's hot candle wax that I'm remembering and it smells sweet. I haven't connected these with anything that triggers them yet, but I could be in my car, in my front yard, in my bed, at work, or anywhere. My dreams, too, are affected by my past. Sometimes I have dreamt of my being able to stand up to people. But other times I would be kissing someone while they are lying on top of me, or they are just on top of me and I can't breathe. And then just as I am "waking up" in my nightmare—I assume it's my husband—but as the person leaves and I catch up with him, I see it's my brother and he's crying.

I used to go out drinking and hit walls until my knuckles would swell and bleed just so I'd distract myself for a little while from my emotional pain. And I used to obsess about things. It would take forever to write about all the things I obsessed about. I focused on friendships, even in grade school, boyfriends, my husband, and even food. If I didn't have a problem to obsess about, I'd start worrying and create a problem. At one point in my life I even contemplated suicide. I felt so dirty, used, ashamed, and hurt. Sometimes despair and hopelessness were hard to deal with. But I never really tried to do anything. I decided that suicide is messy and that God doesn't make mistakes. I figured that I must be here for a good reason. Besides, I haven't met my children yet. When I have children I know that my family will be different, better. I will speak the truth to my children at the level of their understanding.

Now, today, I have a hard time with my life being so calm. Sometimes I still slip back into my old ways. It was very hard for me to let my husband really know me. I couldn't be myself. Hell, I didn't even know who I was. As I am working through all these things so far, my husband hasn't left me, nor have my friends. I am beginning to understand my father's illness and the family system that worked with it. But it has taken *a lot* of hard work. I know I still have a lot more work to do, because each time I get by one issue from the past a new one pops up. I just feel there is so much more I'm not ready for yet, but I know now that there are more opportunities for me to learn through dealing with these difficulties. I know that God loves me and I want to know more. I am growing and changing. I have changed 180 degrees in two years time.

I look to the future with a lot of joy from raising my own family I'd like to end my story at this point by summing up my life with a paragraph that best illustrates how my childhood affected my life overall: At first it stifled the real me as I began to develop. I stumbled on a lot of things in life which made me strong. I think I gained a lot of insight which I would normally not have gotten. I get a second childhood now to discover what I like and who I am. I'm a very open-minded person and willing to try anything. I tend to get very blue at times, but I know the way out now. I can't wait to see what's next!

EVIL AND SIN ARE IGNORANCE
ACTED UPON

Up until the age of four this forty-one-year-old European American, lesbian woman describes her family as being "normal" and happy. Then the birth of her sister changed her mother into a stranger. Both daughters were emotionally and physically abused. Her sister became an alcoholic to escape from their childhood trauma, while this woman believes she developed a multiple personality disorder to survive:

Life was fine until I was four. My mother then had a difficult pregnancy with my sister. She was very sick most of the time. After my sister was born, my mother changed into a stranger. She became mean and cruel. She ridiculed my sister and me in every way possible. She destroyed our self-esteem. My sister is a recovering alcoholic who left the family eight years ago. I left it only one year ago. Two years ago I went into therapy because I kept feeling like I needed to cry very hard and didn't know why.

My mother was so cruel that everyone in the family was afraid of her. She controlled everyone including adult relatives, teachers, and family friends to the extent that they pretended everything was okay. I was very deeply ashamed of the "wrongness" in our family. I kept it secret for that reason. Of course, she made us afraid to get help from "outsiders." We got into trouble if our teachers liked us or if some adult took an interest in us. If people did try to help us, we were punished harder. So no one helped us, not even our grandparents. If they were visiting and my mother started in on me, they went out and sat in their car so they wouldn't have to see or hear it. My mother's father knew my mother was sick and he did nothing. My father took her side, too. I wish my father and grandfather had talked to my mother and forced her into therapy.

When I was a child she was physically cruel as well. She cared more about appearances and being proper than about enjoying life. She *never* praised us. She taught us how to doubt ourselves and hate ourselves. I felt like people looked at my sister and me with great pity. I was ashamed to come from such a cruel family. I thought the world was an ugly place, out to get me.

Although I didn't realize what was happening to me as a child, my therapist confirmed that I developed a multiple personality disorder to survive my childhood. I lived in a fantasy world. I would "go away" when things got too hard. I would be aware my mother was beating me or asking me questions that had no answers, but I was only aware enough to know when it was over so I could "come back." As I had no one to talk to I made up "people" in my mind. Some of my other "parts" are loving and helpful and took care of me when I was very sad. As I was growing up I did have friends and I could go to their houses to spend the night and be free for awhile. These times really gave me a breather so I could relax and be myself for a little while.

I read books voraciously as a child. My favorites were Bible stories and the gospel teachings which helped me a lot. I dearly loved Jesus and would fantasize that I was alive in those days. I believed that Jesus would love me even though I was taught by my mother that I was unlovable and a failure. He felt like a secret friend. Who knows, maybe he really did help me. As an adult I looked and looked for help. Church didn't help so I got fed up with organized religion and set out to explore spirituality on my own in a way I could live what I learned.

Finally, I found metaphysics and it helped a lot. I found a book called *A Course in Miracles* that changed everything. I believe in re-incarnation. I believe I must have chosen this life with its painful childhood so that I could learn to sharpen my skills and be able to learn valuable lessons of overcoming my limitations and self-doubt. I believe it strengthened me and taught me that I am strong and it taught me how to use my "extra senses." I understand people well. I am a good judge of character and have a lot of compassion for others. Now and as a child I had a strong moral code that I followed which was to do no harm to others as best I could manage. For my profession I chose to become a nurse to help people who were underdogs like me. I now am a staff RN in a small rural hospital where I give nursing care to four to seven patients.

Before metaphysics, but as an adult, I thought I was crazy. I had all these negative conversations in my head and I was suicidal frequently. I hoped I could die by just laying down and going to sleep. When that didn't happen I hit myself and stuck needles into my arms. I would pull my hair and bang my head. I felt that if I could get others all riled up they wouldn't notice my faults. But my feelings of worthlessness and hopelessness were so great I thought I would never be able to get through it. I also behaved oddly at times, like a child. Finally, I decided that suicide would be a blessed end to unbearable pain. I sat with a hunting knife trying to get up enough courage to stab myself in the heart. Failing at that I bought a gun and played Russian Roulette.

It was four years ago that I found out about metaphysics. It took me two years after that to realize that I needed counseling. I found a therapist who gave me a correct diagnosis, multiple personality disorder, and is teaching me how to integrate my other selves. When I found out that I had multiple personalities I couldn't breathe, my body went numb and weak. I felt like I would throw up. One year into counseling I knew I had to tell my mother to get out of my life. I walked away from my entire family, except for my sister. I have no interest in being with them because none of them wants to get involved, and besides, they "love" my parents. Since then I have felt like I've been let out of prison. Even though I was once suicidal, I now feel that there is always a way to get help. If I run into an adult who needs help with a traumatic past I encourage them to go into therapy and read books on the subject. I would also try to be unconditionally loving, but keep healthy boundaries.

There are several codependency groups and an Adult Children of Alcoholics group here where I live, and I've been to ten-plus meetings and one year of group therapy. I went to hear that I was not the only one. I went to learn to release the shame where it was safe to do so. I also attended a parent class for people in recovery. The meetings were always deeply painful. I cried and relived the trauma every time, but they have really helped. As my self-image improved I was better able to see that I'm not the only one with troubles. I assumed that everyone was selfish and cruel and given enough time they would hurt me. Now I don't take things personally like I used to. I trust people more.

Growing up and graduating from high school helped to make things better for me. I could then go away to school. Later I went into the Army to get even further away. But while I was in school as a child it was a pretty negative experience for me. Because of my poor self-image, my teachers didn't like me and reinforced my mother's messages about my lack of self-worth. I did have one science teacher in the seventh grade that liked me and told me I was too smart to be getting Cs and Bs in her class. I ended up with an A in her class.

Schools see kids several hours of the day. If teachers were better trained, in psychology for one thing, they could cue in quicker to children that need help. There should be a way to screen for children in dysfunctional, harmful homes. These children need someone to talk to. Abusive parents should be reported—for both physical and emotional abuse—to the proper authorities. The targeted families should then be required to go through an education process to teach parents how to raise their children with kindness. Those who refuse to cooperate should have their children taken away from them. Parenting classes should be an ongoing project.

Marriage looked like a nightmare to me, but I did get married once. I'm now divorced. I didn't want children for a long time, but I had a pair of twin girls who are now 13. I started having trouble dealing with them when they were around five years of age. I, too, abused my children. I was scared that my kids would be taken away from me. It took me years to find someone I trusted to help us. I believe that family problems do get passed on if the pattern isn't consciously disrupted. With therapy, parenting classes, good support, and honest discussions with my children, I can keep from continuing the vicious cycle. I now have given them information about abuse, my own childhood abuse, and admitted my guilt to them. They forgave me. They also accept my reasons for not being around my parents, their grandparents. We are in family therapy and we talk openly about *all* issues with no repercussions for fair, honest sharing. I have now allowed my daughter's friends to live with us temporarily when things were rough at home for them.

Oddly enough, my mother did teach me some valuable things. One thing she taught me was that women are strong and capable. Although she went a little overboard, I did grow up respecting women and I became an independent person. After counseling I was able to discover that I am a lesbian and that it is okay. I was able to go after a dream I've had for years and be successful at it. I started a newsletter and a support group for the gay and lesbian community here. I volunteer for a rape relief group 48 hours a month, and also for an AIDS volunteer group. After my therapist confirmed my trauma as real, I became more comfortable talking about my past. Talking about it helps me continue to heal and I am able to help my friends by sharing my experiences, and I encourage them to try counseling.

In my past I had a lot of pain along the way. Remembering the pain and isolation and dealing with my own children brings up those painful memories. Confusion caused problems and pain in many of my relationships before I got help. I still have a fear of intimacy, and I am claustrophobic and have an exaggerated startle response. I also think daily about my childhood experiences, and I go to therapy sessions weekly. But I'd say it actually has affected me both negatively and positively, all things considered.

On the positive side, learning to trust myself and rise above hardship is a joyful experience. I have learned to let myself grieve and cry for myself, and I share those experiences with my therapist. I am also learning to accept consolation and comfort from others. My communication skills were sharpened due to my not having anyone to listen to me or to validate me as a child. I just kept trying to say it clearer and better. It has also made me acutely aware of human rights issues and *real* family values. And I feel far less judgmental than my peers, because I have been on the bottom and know I have worth and value. I have empathy and understanding of others' problems. So, I'm not sorry for anything that happened to me or how I turned out. I am stronger for the experience.

I have learned that human beings are good at heart. That "evil" and "sin" are *ignorance* acted upon. That the pain and sickness can stop with me. My children have a better chance than I did. I have also learned that forgiveness is extremely important in healing. It shouldn't be done too soon though, you should express your pain and anger at what happened to you. Then when you have emptied out, then forgiveness can heal, even if the parents like mine are out of reach. By forgiving them and having empathy for them, I can forgive myself for my own faults. I am innocent and not a failure. I am talented and have a lot to offer my community.

I am living the way I want to, making my own choices, not based on image or appearances but based on what feels right to me. Even though new issues keep coming up I know how to deal with them now when I didn't before. I know because I can still be triggered into old habits. The difference is I now have a choice of actions. I enjoy my work very much and I feel success in it. The feedback I get today from my friends and acquaintances tells me I am okay. What's really important is that I know I am improving and not only am I "normal," I am exceptional. I have a good therapist and new friends with whom my mother would disapprove of heartily.

I know all sides of the issues. I know how to listen, and by dealing with my own pain I don't pass it along to others. My contributions are positive. I am better able to see the good in others, too. I am able to love the so-called unlovables in our society. I have the energy and the desire to pass along the love and support I've received in my recovery, to help others in theirs. I have learned what unconditional love *really* is. I look to the future to bring me more and more discovery and growth. I never want to stop growing and learning.

Chapter 6

Pariah or Paragon

We found that people who experienced a traumatic childhood came from all kinds of families. Many participants noted that they were viewed by outsiders as outcasts or pariahs in society. They were poor or drunkards with whom no one wanted to associate. Other participants said their families were seen by outsiders as perfect or paragons in society, in that they were churchgoing, leaders in the community, and/or wealthy.

The first two stories are examples of outsiders viewing the families as pariahs in society. The participant in the first story was in foster care because his father was unknown and his mother was in a mental asylum. The welfare system referred to the siblings as "problem children." The second story is about a participant whose father was an alcoholic and the family was very poor. The children in the family were referred to as "the crazy Gene Sorenson kids."

The family in the third story was church going and seen as a paragon in society. The father was one of the highest paid people in the county and the mother was a supportive housewife. These parents were seen as community leaders. Community members did not intervene, either because they did not know the abuse was occurring or because they did not want to get involved.

NOTHING IS AS IMPORTANT AS LOVING SOMEBODY AND HAVING SOMEBODY LOVE YOU

This is the story of a fifty-one-year-old European American male who works thirty-five to forty hours a week as a cook and with a

Surviving and Transcending a Traumatic Childhood
© 2007 by The Haworth Press, Inc. All rights reserved.
doi:10.1300/5839_06

cleaning crew. He has been married once but is now divorced and has no children. He and his siblings were raised in foster homes most of their childhood. His early life was one of abandonment, alienation, discrimination, emotional abuse, mental illness, physical abuse, and poverty:

Answering your questions has been quite an emotional thing for me. It helped me to uncover some anger that is still there after all these years. Actually, I'm not surprised, as I am really being informed when I think through and answer these questions. That is good, not bad.

For a long time I did not feel good about me—maybe for about 20 years. Then, only after studying psychology and related sciences did I come to really like me very much. I am quite a sensitive person. I certainly would not admit to that if I was 22 years old. There is wisdom in maturity.

I am a middle born. I have three older siblings, two sisters and one brother, and one brother born one year and nine months to the day younger than me, to whom I am closest. My mother was put in an insane asylum when I was very young. She died when she was 70 in a nursing home. I don't know if my father is living or not. I don't have a pressing need to know, really, but I am interested. Anyway, my traumatic times were from the ages of 6 to 17.

My early life seems to be a blur of being constantly put in one foster home after another with a few really bad experiences standing out in my mind. Two or three school changes are about normal for most people, but I went to 9 different schools and lived in 11 different foster homes. It seems that I would just start school and begin to make friends, then I'd be uprooted and moved to another home and school district. I would never reveal to my other classmates that I was in a foster home' cause they would know I was not from a "normal" home. It was at this time in answering this questionnaire that I thought, now, all of a sudden I don't find this questionnaire all that easy to fill out. It's 23 pages long on both sides of the paper. So sometimes I had to stop and leave the questions alone for awhile, and then I'd come back to it when I could handle it again.

Anyway, I remember one instance when I was seven years old and I was in a foster home. For some reason I got in his truck and was messing around with its horn until I fucked it up. It had that big button that you pushed to honk it. Well, it came loose, so I pulled on the spring that was under it until the horn continued to beep, only stopping when the battery was depleted. I, of course, had no knowledge of what I had really done at seven years of age. When Mr. Kingsley, the foster parent, came home and found out that I was the one to f— up his truck he started throwing me from one couch to the other. I sure am glad now that cement benches weren't invented yet. Now, here I go again, I had to throw this questionnaire aside again because some of these memories are still so powerful.

As I was able to start writing again I turned the page to hopefully find more space to go on with my answer to this question, but instead I found another question. Listen, I'm not done with question #16 yet. Brevity has its place, I guess.

When I was about 12 or 13 and in the foster home of an old woman of about 50, she told my brother and me that the Highland Welfare Department had said that we were "problem children." Well, after hearing that a few times, my brother and I proved them right. I think we exceeded their expectations in that regard. Boy, were we two little bastards you would want to meet! See how that one statement just told a few times affected our self-esteem.

I think you should never say to your children that they are stupid or dumb or no good. Children like to please adults and also like to make sure that mom and dad are right. Call them stupid, or tell them enough times that they won't amount to anything and they will make you right. If I could advise parents on how to treat their children I would say that I don't think it would matter how they disciplined their child, but that they must include that child back in the family soon. Whether it be in the next half an hour or the next day I don't care, but they should tell that child that they still really love them and always will. Yes, of course there are going to be times they may dislike that child or what they do, but they as their parent will also enjoy hugging and loving them no matter what.

It was at the age of 13 that I was sent to see a psychiatrist because of aggressive behavior. He told me that perhaps I would end up like my mother who went nuts and was put in St. John's Mental Institution. It wasn't until I was 17 and in the 11th grade that the turning point in my life came. I was put in a mental institution for 364 days. I learned so much there about what crazy really means. I still read any article or book about mental illness because I find it fascinating. Also, the study of psychology and, of course, its related sciences such as psychoanalysis and the psychology of handwriting and color interpretation are what I feel allowed me to transcend my personal difficulties. What made this time especially hard though was that I and another kid that some "others" deemed "not right in the head" had to ride the regular school bus. The other kids on the bus, including the doctor's kids, got off at the public school, while the two of us got to go on to the mental institution. Ain't that special? I had to leave this question for awhile at this point so I could change my mood.

No one person stands out at all in my mind as being a key person to helping me survive and transcend my childhood. Well, maybe one, Mrs. Jacobs. She one time beat the hell out of me because I busted up everything in my room at her house. She did a good job. I was, of course, involved with the welfare agency people a lot in my childhood. All I can say about them is that they did a good job of ignoring my foster home situations, mostly because they probably didn't want to erode the fragile system that they had already.

You asked me who I wished could have helped me. Well, let's see . . . maybe Elvis Presley. FUCK YOU! There was nobody there to help me or to listen to me. I just kept being put into another foster home which always made the situation worse. I just wished that someone close to me could have said, "Hey, no matter what, I love you." But, there was nobody.

When I think back about my school experiences I can say that they had sort of a positive, but mostly negative, influence on my life. It was important for me to be with other kids my age, but sometimes I had bad experiences with some of them. Like when they'd slap my school books out of my arms because I'd be carrying them a certain way and they'd say, "Don't carry those books like a girl!" School was always another new situation that I also had to adjust to, which was good and bad. One thing this did for me is that I sure adapt quickly today to new situations.

When I was in school, I didn't even have the confidence that I would graduate from high school. I know now that I was a lot smarter than I thought at the time. I just wish somebody would have instilled that confidence in me. The school administrators were no help to me either, as I'm sure they didn't know what was really going on with me. In general, school was real hard for me because the other students were aware that I was not from a "normal" father-mother relationship.

Something schools could do is teach classes on being a successful parent. There are lots of kids out there who could sure benefit from such teaching, and it just might help to keep some kids from having to become foster children. Schools should also show that love knows no boundaries. Above all, hug the children. But, you shouldn't say that you love all the children when you actually do not, and you shouldn't say it even if you really do love a particular child. And I make a distinction here between love and sexual love.

When someone has a problem I listen with the third ear. If I were to make a suggestion as to how to help a child going through a stressful time I would say, hug her or him. Tell them you really love them, no matter what. Tell them again that no matter what, you will still love them, then, hug them again. And if this person that needs help is now an adult that went through a bad childhood, know that an adult still has the hurt child inside of them even though they may have gotten bigger on the outside. The adult still needs to be loved and hugged. Be sure and hug old people, too, for nothing is as important as loving somebody and having people love you. Always remember if you cannot love your family, love another human being. I love to love. I am quite sensitive, but I don't let that get me into situations that will prove difficult.

You asked if I am comfortable talking about my childhood. Well, it depends on whom I'm talking to. A faceless, out-of-maybe-nowhere person I find easier to talk to than one-on-one in a restaurant—a lot easier. Of course, it has gotten easier to talk about my past since the age of 40. I'm 51 now and when you reach 40, if one is so lucky, one looks back and the introspection becomes a big deal. I like it. I've never felt the need to see a counselor though. I feel there is a stigma attached to seeing one. Why do you need to see any counselor anyway? I healed myself. I always knew that no matter what, somehow, some way I would make it.

My childhood experiences seem to have weakened my spiritual beliefs and they changed when I found out that there is not an Easter bunny. I don't believe that there is such a thing as God. If there is one, he must have been on vacation having sex with some sexy angels when I could have used his help. I feel that if you have a lot of money then the "church" welcomes you with a pew, maybe even one named in your honor.

Boy, you asked a lot of questions!

The vicious cycle in my family seems to be divorce. I've been married once and divorced once. I won't fall into this cycle again, however, because I won't get married anymore. I have been in three long-term committed relationships though. So I know I can have close relationships with other people. It's not easy, however. It's slow, real slow. My childhood experiences affected my later sexual life also, I believe, because I lacked a father-figure type person in my life. I mean, I had just about none. I am very careful who I call a friend versus an acquaintance. But, if I make a friend, not an acquaintance, that friend is around for a long time.

I actually don't think about my bad times that much anymore. Certain seasons or times of the year may stir things up in my mind a little though. And I still have about two or three flashbacks a year when something on TV or perhaps a court appearance triggers it. But, I never tried to hurt myself because of my past because I don't like pain. And I never tried to commit suicide over it. Why should you quit life so soon? Unfortunately, I'm not close to my brothers or sisters because of our childhood. But, my older sister and her husband were quite influential to me at one time. My sister is an honest person and her husband is an honest and a loving man.

At one time, maybe more, I felt that perhaps I deserved what I was getting. I was wrong. I deserved so much better. I also used to blame my mother, my father, and the welfare agency for my problems. But, if you are always thinking bad thoughts, wanting revenge, to hurt someone or even kill someone, etc., then these thoughts can intrude on you at any time, for any length of time. If they do for more than an hour then you may be cutting into fully 50 percent of your own happiness. You cannot be happy if you are thinking bad thoughts. Because my childhood was the mold that formed me into what I am today, it wasn't until I had the maturity of thought that I was able to make some changes for the better in myself. I know now that I cannot change anybody, but I can change me. Today I know that I haven't resolved all the issues from my childhood, as I'm still trying to do it. But, the older I get the better I am getting at doing it.

I am an attention-grabbing person. I've been at it for about 40 years. I can get attention anytime I want. I'm really good at it. But, I'm not so self-centered that I don't let others have center stage when they need it, because I have the innate capacity to get attention whenever I want. I'm not selfish. I like to make other people laugh, whether they laugh at me or with me, so long as they laugh. The clown gets more attention than the nonclown. Yes, now that you ask, I do wear torn blue jeans that are tight, and I wear spandex underneath in bright colors: red, yellow, or blue. I also may be naked underneath. Of course, we as adults know when someone else is doing something just to get attention. I know people know that. I *still* love to do it. But, I also think deeply about things like prejudice, racism, biases, and what I can do to make it better.

Because of what happened to me in my childhood and what I have learned through my survival, I have these feelings about life: Life is. Life is not fair or foul. Life is. What a person thinks, what a person says, and what a person says he or she will do, that becomes your own destiny. No one, I mean no one else decides your own destiny but yourself. I look to a future of more happiness but some sadness, too, with the passing or rather the continued journey of my friends.

THE SCHOOL KIDS CALLED US "THE CRAZY GENE SORENSON KIDS"

Even at age seventy-five, this European American woman still vividly remembers the challenges of growing up in a home with poverty, alcoholism, suicide, and being treated like an outcast:

My father immigrated to America from Sweden in about 1903 because there was no work in Sweden. He came alone at about age 25. My mother was born on a farm in the United States. They met when they both worked as hired help on a farm. They fell in love and married. At that time they were both about 34 years of age. My father got a job as a tailor and I have been told that he was the best one in the community. Despite being married to my mother he was lonesome for his relatives who were still in Sweden, and he started drinking alcohol. He purchased a new home and new furniture. I was born in this home, the youngest of four girls. I remember when I was three years old, I saw him come home under the influence of alcohol and it was the beginning of a real nightmare. He acquired friends who encouraged such a habit. There was not much help, then, in the 1920s. We lost our home and furniture and had to move into an old house. Things went from bad to worse after that. My brother was born shortly thereafter. He was a Down syndrome baby. Those were the days you hid such a person. The doctor told my mother that he would probably live to 12 or 13 years of age so she insisted on taking care of him. My mother was a fine Christian woman and made the best home she could for us, under the circumstances. By that time I was in school. We never dared to ask our friends to our home because of my brother and my father. My father was drinking heavily by now, which made us very poor.

One day my father left the house and said to my mother, "I'm going now, and if I find you let the children starve, I'll come back and persecute you." He then went into the garage and shot himself, but he aimed for his heart and got his arm instead. My mother called the police and they took him to the hospital. After a week, they transferred him to a detox station, which was a place for the inebriates and mentally ill. We visited him, but us kids were afraid of him. He developed gangrene in his arm and the pain was so intense. They didn't have drugs to fight it then, so the night before Easter Sunday he hung himself and died. At his funeral I was nine. I didn't know whether to be happy or relieved. While my dad was ill at the state hospital the kids at school called us "the crazy Gene Sorenson kids." This was very hard to take.

After this we were very poor for a long time before we got welfare. Then it was 60 dollars a month for the six of us. My mom was destitute and sent us out with little notes to beg for anything. I wish that more people would have helped us out with more food and clothes without our begging for it, but I wish even more that people would have befriended us. We worked at all kinds of jobs to make money. I never got a dime for myself after I hit eighth grade. I had to pay for my own school supplies, dentist bills, and clothes. Most of our clothes were given to us by caring people, but of course I wasn't dressed in the current "fad" clothes.

My mother believed in prayer and spent much time on her knees for the welfare of her children. I feel that it was God's leading that sent us to the old house that we moved into. Next door to us were girls of our age and they went to our church, First Baptist. Even though the church looked down on us because we were a drunkard's kids, these girls became our friends and we felt accepted by them so that we slowly emerged from our inferiority complex.

One of my friends quit school in the ninth grade. I thought, why not me? We were so poor that I couldn't dress as every one else and our poverty made it hard to study properly. Schools really should do something to make the poor kids feel important enough to be elected to different clubs and offices. As it was then, we poor kids really took a back seat in school activities. But, I was determined to get an education and I did make some good friends in school. I graduated from high school and went to Iowa City to work and go to night school. With no money for college I returned to Grantsburg and worked in a large department store. I then started dating a boy who was living with his aunt. She was not an easy person for him to live with.

After he became a Christian we got married. We were fairly young and we got married to get away from his aunt. We got along beautifully because he converted. He then started to sell insurance. It was very rough going at first, but this week we are celebrating our 50th year in what has become a very successful business. When we first started out we purchased a bank building to use and we are still there today. We are now retired but sold the business to our son, who also taught school for 10 years.

My husband and I have been very active in the church where he was even a deacon. We have four wonderful children who are all dedicated Christian adults now. I credit knowing the Lord and finding strength in my Christian life as the key factor in my surviving and transcending a traumatic early life. My religion gave me much comfort and guidance in my early years. It also gave me strength to go on, as I knew that God was watching over me and taking care of me. My mom and all my sisters have been good Christian people, and the church programs were especially helpful to me as they helped me to make new friends.

My wonderful husband of 53 years also has made me feel important. Since we've been together I have become more confident and secure and able to talk about my early years. One thing I learned from my past is to never take a drink of any alcoholic beverages. I still see that as the cause of my dad's tragedy. Therefore, I believe that you can make a go of it if you make the right choices in life and depend on God's leading. Although I can still feel a little inferior at times I know that life is not always easy, but in God's hands you are safe. The Lord says to forgive 70 × 7, and that's the rule I live by.

One thing I am very proud of is the fact that my husband and I have helped many hurting people in the years we've been married. We took in kids who needed a home while they were going to college. We also made a home for a foster boy who had alcoholic parents. We have tried to be good Christian people by helping those in need.

I now live in a lovely home and have many wonderful friends. God has been good!!

YOU CAN BE THE SUM OF YOUR OWN CHOICES AND NOT THE PRODUCT OF YOUR PAST

When he was fifteen, this forty-year-old European American man shot his father. The policeman who picked him up after the shooting told him he was not a bad person or a sinner, and promised he would help him in life any way he could. The policeman kept his promise. Today, in honor of the policeman who saw some good in him, the man has become a policeman himself:

My father took out his frustrations by beating people. He had two favorite targets, my mother and me. This was not just hitting, he would beat on my mother for what seemed like hours. He started beating on me when I was 14 years old. I had been beaten before many times, but I can remember that it changed around age 14 to me being a direct target rather than incidental. I had started to rebel and tried to protect my younger brothers and older sister. I remember hiding in my room. I would get between the mattress and bed springs and wrap towels and pillows and blankets around my head. I tried to get away from the sounds of my parents screaming and the sounds of my mother getting beaten. I knew my sister would be in her room doing the same thing.

My family went to church twice every Sunday along with Sunday School, catechism, youth night, and choir practice. It seemed like we were always in church. My father was head of the businessmen's league. He was the manager of the local factory and had the highest payroll in the county. I've been told he was one of the highest paid people in the area. Mother was the supportive housewife, as far as the outside world saw. My sister was on the honor roll and a model student.

What the world saw of me was a kid who ran with the local hoods and dressed like a hood and got into fights. I was always trying to prove myself with my fists. When I was 15, a senior boy informed me that my sister was a whore. Even though he was 40 pounds heavier than me, I had a fight with him in an alley behind the post office. I made it a point to not only beat him but humiliate him as well. Afterward his older brother came to my house looking for me. My father said he would take care of the problem. I got beaten by my father. I have scars on my back that still show from this beating. He used an electric extension cord. The cord ripped my skin and raised welts. He made me stand against the wall and "take my beating like a man."

My sister told me that it didn't matter. She said she was bigger than our father and bigger than the town, and that she was going to have a family that loved one another. That was the year she moved away. She never got one cent of financial help from my parents, but she went to college and teaches high school kids science and computers. She married a man while she was in the Peace Corps. They adopted kids. I know she is a happy person. She told me she feels she's had a good life.

After my sister left, things got worse. I was afraid to come home most of the time. I never knew what my father's mood would be. Sometimes he was okay and other times he was furious with my mother and me. You never really knew what was making him mad. He would say it was something you did or said, but I always felt it was not really me. I would spend two or three days away from the house at a time. I lived in barns or stayed at other kids' homes. In those days most of the farms around the area were small dairies. I could get up in the hay above the milkers and stay warm. I would clean up at school in gym or after football practice. I could never figure out why no one asked me about why I was always bruised or why I had welts on my back and legs.

Our town was only about 2,000 people. I felt that there were people who knew what was going on at our house, but chose not to do anything. My mother usually had marks that showed. I remember her telling a neighbor that she had walked into a door and blackened her eye.

There was never any alcohol in the house. I don't ever remember smelling booze on his breath. We did not live in poverty. He should have had no financial worries. But apparently he did have stress and he took it out on us rather than whatever person or demons in his mind caused his problems.

My sister came home from college and took me to our preacher. He said he could not come to our home and talk to our parents unless he was asked by our parents. He said to "Honor your mother and father." He also told us to pray and God would take care of us. We went down the street and talked to the other minister in town. He said we were not in his congregation. He told us he could not help us unless our parents came to him for help. He also told us to pray. I feel to this day that most ministers are full of shit. We begged ministers for help and they refused. This was also the year my youngest brother was born. I don't know anything about him. I knew him that first year of his life, and I've never been around him since. My other brother was ten years old then.

It was early November. There had been trouble at my house. The time period between my father's rages had decreased, before we had weeks and months of relative calm. By calm I mean no beatings or fights, just fear. Now, however, one episode blended to the next. I had come home from school and could hear my mother screaming as I approached the house. It was not just a fight, I could hear her getting hit. I left without going in and stayed away three days. I can't remember where I stayed on this occasion. I was still going to school during the days, sleeping where it was warm at night. I was worried about my ten-year-old brother. But I was not worried in the way you might think. He had told me that mother needed to get hurt because she would not be good. That worried me.

After the third day I came back to the house. I was very cold. I had gotten wet. I walked into the back door of the house and it was so very quiet. I don't know what had been going on the three days I had been gone. I was sure that the one incident had ended and another had begun. When I walked into the kitchen, I saw my mother lying on her back on the kitchen floor. Her glasses were on her face, but the glass lenses were broken. She had blood running out of her nose and onto the floor. She was awake and I could see her eyes following me, but she did not say anything. My father was standing over her. He was sweating and panting like he had been running a race. I hit him from behind. I hit him below the ear. I was trying to kill him. He went down on one knee. He did not go out. He put his hand up to his head. I knew I had hurt him. He looked at me and said, "You'll be sorry you did that."

I ran into the basement where my room was located. I saw that my 10-year-old brother was on the floor behind the bed. He had a blanket wrapped around his head and his hands over his ears. I locked the door and put a chair against it. I unraveled my brother's head. I told him that if father tried to come in and get us that I would kill him. My brother said he would have to warn my father that I was going to kill him or my father would kill my brother. I told my brother that I would tie him up, that way he would not have to tell father. If I failed, my brother would not be blamed. I wrapped the blanket around him so that he looked tied up. I think about this now and think how stupid this thinking was. But you have to remember that we were 10 and 15 years old.

While the conversation was going on with my brother, we could hear our parents starting to scream at each other. Then I heard father coming down the stairs. I loaded my 22-caliber rifle. I waited. He came to the door and was screaming for me to open the door. Then he started to break it in. It was a hollow-frame door. He ran his fist through the door and opened the lock. He pushed the chair away and came into the room. I shot him in the chin. His head spun away and I shot again and struck him in the side of the head. I then shot a third time into his chest. He stood and looked at me. There was no more rage in his face. He said, "You shot me." He then turned and walked out of the bedroom.

My brother was sitting on the floor wrapped in the blanket. His eyes were open. He had seen me shoot his father. He did not look scared, he was not crying, he did not look surprised. I don't think he has ever gotten over what happened. He hates me today. He went to a foster family. He strangled their pet rabbits. I opened the window and crawled out of the house. I left the gun on the ground by the house and walked away.

I don't know why, but I had taken my coat off when I had loaded the gun. It was snowing. I walked out of town towards the next town. We lived on the plains and you could see the lights of the next town even though it was nine miles away. I walked along the railroad tracks toward those lights. I could hear the ambulance siren and the police car. Then they ran the siren to summon the volunteer firemen. I think that was to get people together to look for me.

I continued walking along the tracks. I remember that I wondered why I wasn't crying. I thought I would be killed when the police found me. I wished they would hurry up, but I did not walk to the road for them to find me. About one mile outside of the next town I stopped. I had never really prayed in the years we were going to church. After all, why would God care about some kid? I prayed that night. I prayed that I had not killed my father. I told God that I would never ask him for anything or try to contact him again, if he would only let my father live. (I broke that promise once when I asked God to let my wife live during childbirth.)

I got to the next town and went to the public phone booth. I dialed the operator, told her my name, and told her they needed to send a policeman to the phone booth. A lone policeman arrived. He pulled up right in front of the phone booth. I was so cold. He didn't even get out of the car. He rolled down the window and asked if I was the person who called. He told me to get in and he drove me to the sheriff's office. No handcuffs. He didn't touch me. He didn't even really talk to me. He didn't say whether or not my father was dead. I found out the next day.

I spent the next couple of months in a mental hospital for evaluation. I went to court and was told that I had been charged with attempted murder. I was found not guilty. The judge said people have a right to defend themselves, and that included children.

I believe that if I had not shot my father, I would have grown up like my father. What I do know is that I did not continue to live in fear every day.

When I was arrested, I was taken to the sheriff's office and lodged at the jail. He had a deputy that talked to me, interviewed me regarding the case. He told me that he knew that I was not a bad kid. I don't think anyone had ever said anything like that to me before. I believed he was sincere. He told me he would do everything he could to help me, and he kept his promise. He was killed two years later while driving a 15-year-old arsonist to get a mental health evaluation when he rolled the patrol car. Until that time I really thought that most homes were like mine. After I was arrested I was told otherwise.

After my release from the mental facility and being released from jail, I was placed in an aunt's home, more religion and prayer. She had a white house, white furniture, and white carpet and 10 hours of church per week. She had piped in music and played religious music all day. It was like living in a funeral home. Living there was worse than dying. I was hanging out at the pool hall and getting stoned on cough medicine and beer almost every night. I lived there for six months. I was failing all my classes in school. I got paid a visit by a social worker. He had been asked to visit me by the deputy sheriff. This social worker was trying a new program. He felt that if he could get a troubled kid away from his destructive environment the kid might have a chance to change, that is if the kid had the desire to help himself. This was different from the commonly held beliefs about foster care that they should focus on restoring the family. Why put a kid back into a home when you know that it is going to fail. The social worker had located a home that was almost 200 miles away. My aunt does not understand, to this day, why I wanted to move away from family. There was not really a choice. As long as I was hanging around the same kids and reminded daily by family that I was trouble, then I was going to be trouble.

I met the foster parents. It was not love at first sight. They were young and idealistic and miles out in the country. The thing that stands out in my mind after all these years is that they were always willing to listen to me. I could get up in the middle of the night and they would sit up and let me talk. Sometimes, when I felt bad, I would sit by their bed and talk and cry until I was able to sleep. We talked while we worked. I was able to work after school and on weekends on the farm. I was paid for my work. They showed me that I had value. We went to church, but they talked openly that they did not buy everything they were told, and you had to make up you own mind about what you believed or did not believe. They showed me that you could disagree and not hate the person with whom you disagreed. They showed me that a man and a woman can be friends. They did not let me run around. They did not tolerate my drinking. They made me let them know where I was going, who I was with, and when I would be home. This all let me know they cared about me. Now, 24 years later, they are still my friends. They are still people I can talk to when I have a good story to tell, or a problem to share.

The foster care placement was miles from my home town, away from family and friends, was critical to my recovery. They were good people who provided positive role models and I was able to start fresh, away from destructive relationships.

People didn't act as if our family was going through trauma until everything came to the violent end. Some didn't seem to want to get involved. For others, it seemed they had these problems in their own lives. Teachers, parents of school friends, police all could have helped, but they didn't. Intervention by police after the first incident would have made things different. After the shooting I was helped by teachers, law enforcement officers, and people who came forward and told me they had been abused.

I don't want to paint too fair a picture or lead you to believe that a couple of years with this family turned my life around entirely. It did refocus my direction and got me started on the right course. It was not the end of my problems. You don't grow up in one year. What I had established was a base that I could return to and focus on when I did have trouble. I was in my late 20s before I could accept my parents as not being my enemies anymore. My first wife and I divorced during this time period. My son chose to come live with me after three years. He said that I was stricter, yelled more, and was always on his case. But he also knew it is because I care about him, and because he felt safe with me.

There were times I felt that if only I could have believed the Bible more or tried harder, I could have been a better son, and there would have been no violence. There were also times I blamed my parents and their parents for what happened. My mother could have protected her children.

I was aware that I needed help and was able to accept that help. I was also able to separate the past, the present, and the future, and deal with each separately. My sister and my foster family had the belief that things could change. One thing that could change is one's outlook on life. They believed that you could be the sum of your own choices and not the product of your past.

I didn't see school as a help. Mostly, I felt school minds were closed minds. My high school football coach had a club called Fellowship of Christian Athletes. He advocated prayer, but taught us how to cheat in a game. This also added to my negative feelings about organized religion. People in schools need to be more involved. If they see a crime, they should report it. Ask a kid if he has a problem. Then ask him again. Kids spend more time in school than anywhere else. It is an adult's responsibility to care for any child in trouble, not just your own but all kids.

There were times when I created chaos. The shooting took place in November and for years I found myself setting up fights with my wife during that time of year. The fights seemed to give me a reason to be unhappy. Yes, I have thought of killing myself. I tried once by eating a bottle of aspirin. I threw up.

I am a police officer. I take pride in the fact that I have few fights, altercations, or complaints from the public. I also have a high arrest record. It is not impossible to have both. I learned that anger can be controlled and your fists do not solve problems. I feel compelled to constantly challenge myself. I could work in a section with little pressure, but I've chosen to be on the emergency services team (SWAT), a bomb technician, and fraud investigation. I worked two years in undercover narcotics operations. I earned a meritorious service award for bravery. I feel I contribute to my society on a daily basis.

I am married to a tolerant, wonderful woman. I have absolute faith in her love. I believe that she and our children and our relationship tell the story of how I was able to transcend a childhood of abuse and neglect. My wife is my best friend. She's also a teacher.

Our home has its problems, but for the most part, I am a relatively happy person. I've learned that I needed to forgive myself for being human. I feel I've survived and transcended. There are no beatings going on in my home. I look forward to my work. I enjoy my family. There are people in my life who have been friends for over two decades. I enjoy hobbies outside of my work. I look forward to more adventures and hearing of the adventures of my children.

Chapter 7

People Who Helped

As we read the participants' stories we found that there were often people who made a difference in their lives as children or in adult-hood—people who helped them survive and helped them on their road to recovery. Sometimes it was a teacher in school or a neighbor who spent time with them in a way that allowed them to "take a vacation" from the abuse. It was someone who befriended them so they could see hope for the future—allowing them to see a world that could be different from what they had experienced.

The two stories in this chapter describe very different kinds of people who had major influences on the lives of abused children. The participant in the first story got "kicked out" of her home when she was sixteen. She then stayed with families of friends while working and going to high school. During her last year of high school, she moved into an apartment and her roommates and friends became her family. They listened to her and did not judge her. They also provided a window into family lives that were "not so fucked up" as the one from which she came. The participant in the second story went around the world to find people who helped him recover as an adult.

As outsiders, we may not know when we are helping someone who is experiencing or has experienced a traumatic childhood. But, from these examples, it is obvious that we can help such a person by being a friend, being supportive, and providing a window to more normal lives that provide hope.

Surviving and Transcending a Traumatic Childhood
© 2007 by The Haworth Press, Inc. All rights reserved.
doi:10.1300/5839_07

I BLAME MY PARENTS, MY BROTHERS, AND GOD

This young European American woman remembers having seventeen pet dogs killed as punishment when she was bad. She would find them in the garbage can. Then she would get a new dog when she was good. She was also sexually abused by her stepbrothers:

I was the youngest of four daughters and am 23 now. My father would threaten my mother with guns and would kill dogs or cats as a way of manipulating members of my family. My mother finally divorced my father shortly after my mother's sister was killed by her husband. Until second grade I lived with my mom and three sisters. We were poor and my mother worked a lot and often went out drinking. My older sisters took care of the other two of us.

Eventually, my mom could not afford to take care of us and my dad had remarried a woman who had four sons. My dad and his wife wanted to take care of us and mom thought it would be best. My stepmother was an evil witch and so were her sons. They provided food and shelter and a hell of a lot of dysfunctional family head games, power trips, and drunken evenings by the television set.

My stepmother was boss of the family. She spoiled her kids who, in turn, were troubled, mean, drug abusers, and in trouble with the law. They were shit heads. Honest to God, we girls were angels but always got punished for something dumb. I remember once my stepmother putting me on a stool, facing the wall until I told her why I never smiled. (I never noticed that I wasn't smiling very often because I had always been straight-faced and not very happy in general.) She yanked on my hair and demanded that I explain why I'm so goddamn unhappy. I felt terrible because I couldn't answer her.

Some of us girls would move back in with mother for a year or so. Then, hating it there with her new alcoholic husband and all, we would move back to dad's house.

I had 17 dogs that I remember. One at a time they were killed by a brother or my dad because "we didn't deserve a pet." They would then treat us with a new one when we were good. The stepbrothers sexually molested me and perhaps my sisters, but at the time I didn't know how bad it was. I liked it because it was the only attention I would get. The things I did to survive included spacing out on television, working on art projects, and eventually moving away. I had no friends in those early childhood years. We lived way out in the country and I felt trapped. I talked to my stuffed rabbit, my dogs, and my sisters. Some of the other things I did which helped me survive were to make fun of how my stepmother acted when she was drunk. I also made fun of the fact that my mother was a religious fanatic and she collected cheap "Jesus stuff." That taught me that my parents' religion was crazy and that I had to develop my own. My sisters and I realized that my parents were just fucked up and there was nothing we could do to change it. I learned from everyone's mistakes and promised myself I would not be that way.

Schools could do more to help children. I enjoyed art classes which I got at school. I think that each child should be taken in to meet a counselor even if the child doesn't do it on their own. Many children do not know that there is help and someone needs to help them communicate early on.

I lived with my mother when I was 15. At 16 I ran away from home, or rather got kicked out. For the first few months away from home I stayed with the families of friends and supported myself by working at McDonalds. I was sick often. Grades were not important but I did well because I took a lot of art classes and art was very important to me. During my last year of high school I had my own apartment and was continually making friends, and roommates became my family. My friends also became a support group for me. I told them about my home life and they were the first people that I spoke to that listened and cared. It made me realize how "fucked up" my families were. The sister closest to me in age had a boyfriend who helped her deal with stuff and together they moved into a new apartment. Both of them helped me tremendously because they had gone through the feelings and treatment from my folks.

My first relationship with a boyfriend was intense and difficult. I immediately grew dependent on him and stuck by him through three years of him cheating on me. It was also a very wonderful relationship at times and we both learned a lot about relationships and love. He was on the verge of being a problem drinker which was a problem to me because I avoided alcohol. The one good thing about our relationship was that we talked in depth about everything. It made me realize that lack of communication is the root of every problem. What makes me happy now is that I learned to pinpoint mistakes and mishaps and I discuss them and learn from them. I actually find humor in the crazy lives that my parents can't help but lead.

My sisters, friends, romantic partners, and counselors helped me in the process of surviving and transcending. I think it also helped me being sent back and forth between my two parents. I learned what was awful about each arrangement. It gave me a chance to step back and remove myself for awhile. I was finally able to move away from both places. If I hadn't gone through such a shitty childhood I would not have learned the skills for dealing with problems and helping others deal with problems. I'm very good at that now.

I blame my father for what had happened to us. He sat dumbly while his wife made our lives hell. I wished, then, that both parents would have gotten help for alcoholism. Today I blame my parents, my brothers, and God. They didn't let me know that I was a decent person. I have tried to forgive and I have tried to forget. I feel both are useless unless the person causing the pain has tried to rehabilitate themselves. I feel it is better to hate the bad parts about people so that you don't put yourself in a position to be hurt again.

When I was 20 I thought I was going crazy. I became very depressed when I broke up with a man. It brought back all sorts of memories and feelings of being helpless as a child. I began seeing a psychiatrist, went on antidepressants, and spent a lot of time reflecting on stuff. I also read books about adult children of alcoholics.

I have thought about committing suicide. I thought if you're not happy, why be here. I sometimes felt like shit. I never did try to kill myself, however. I thought that someday I could just start all over and totally change everything about myself, and try again.

I have close relationships with people now. I attribute that to my ability to communicate. I have never been married but I have been in five long-term relationships. I hated divorce so much that I swore never to get married. I do want a committed relationship, however. I will not have children, but I may adopt. The population is out of control and living in a family with eight kids was ridiculous. Perhaps if there weren't so many children to take care of we would have gotten more attention and had better parent/child relationships.

My childhood affects me in many ways today. Because of the sexual abuse I question my role in sex, and my ability to make decisions about sex. My escape through art forced me to be creative and I use creativity in my life. I am still interested in art and music. I became very skillful in trades that are traditionally male, such as woodworking, welding, and foundry. I also tend to be masculine. I relate this back to being treated unfairly as a girl child as compared to my stepbrothers. I have fears about alcohol consumption because of my parents. I also have ulcers and stomach problems which I attribute to the stress during my childhood. My childhood affected me both positively and negatively in that it made me very compassionate, very understanding, and thoughtful. It also made me bitter, scared, and easily hurt.

I have flashbacks regularly. They are real-life memories such as finding my pet in the garbage can, dead. These flashbacks are triggered when I'm interacting with children, sexual encounters, jobs where the boss gets uptight, holidays, seasonal changes, and being in the house where the abuse happened. I have nightmares of being chased by my stepmother and trying to save myself by scraping her against barbed wire until one of us would die. I also have a recurring dread of being abandoned in a field of daisies. Sometimes I have positive dreams of telling them off. I do this without shaking or crying, but firmly and tactfully telling them what assholes they were.

The future will bring whatever it will bring. I am hoping for a healthy relationship and hope to help children in need. I would like to help in raising neighborhood kids, friends' kids, and relatives' kids because most kids don't have enough adult care. I would also like to teach art to children in hopes of helping them look inward and creatively deal with problems and to keep them from getting to the edge.

I ALMOST DIED BEFORE I REALIZED THAT THE ONLY PERSON ABUSING ME NOW WAS ME

"Life is a process. As long as I am proceeding in life then I will find issues to resolve. The more I uncover, the more I find to discover." So says this fifty-four-year-old European American man who described himself as an emotional wreck until he was in his late thirties due to the emotional and physical abuse he received from his parents and older brother. Once he finally was away from his abusers he almost died before he realized that the only person who was abusing him then was himself. Listen to his story and find out how he finally was

able to overcome his traumatic childhood and then his early adult years of self-abuse:

When I was four, my mother scalded me with hot water in the basement laundry of our home because I was having a temper tantrum. She had done a similar thing to my brother when he was about the same age, but she had used cold water on him. The scalding put me into the hospital for 17 days with third-degree burns on my chest, upper arms, and stomach.

I can remember well the hospital experience. I had an "out-of-body" experience where I was looking down on myself in the emergency room while the doctors and nurses were peeling away my scalded flesh. I remember the bandages sticking to my skin and being scraped off every morning. I remember crying for my parents to stay with me (real sobbing) when they left for home in the afternoons.

I cannot remember the ambulance ride to the hospital, but until I was in my teens, sirens from fire trucks, ambulances, police cars, etc., terrified me. If one went by our home at night, I would run screaming to my father and get in bed with him. It wasn't until I was in my 30s that I was able to overcome my fear of the dark.

Actually, I was an emotional wreck until I was in my 30s. I was out of control and insecure. I was controlled not by logic, or anything positively oriented, but by my emotional outlook. And, my emotional responses to every event retarded my intellect.

By the time I was nine, my parents were told that I needed therapy. They did nothing, however, because they didn't want to let out their secrets: how I was burned when I was four; nor about their continued abuse. For punishment for my many misdeeds mother would switch my legs with branches I had to cut myself. She preferred the ones I made from bamboo as they cut my legs the worst. She also approved of the ones I made from privet hedges. But, any other kind she would often reject and send me back outside to cut a more punishing type of switch.

Father used his belt on me or the back of a hair brush, a silver-wedding present. He used to tell me that he had to use something to hit me with as it hurt his hands too much to not use some type of tool. My father was a Methodist minister. He taught me religion with a belt, a Bible, and a bottle. All of them scarred me.

When you are a small person who is dependent upon others for support and they mistreat you (all the while saying they are doing so because they loved you), life is a confusing place. Home is both pleasure and pain. You never knew at home what was to be dealt out, and it was supposed to be "love" either way. Love, for me, took on a painful interpretation.

My brother beat me as well. Not physically, as my parents, but psychologically. Life was one big put-down from him from my earliest memories. Even now it still is. The only relationship we have, I am 54 and he is 57, is one where he is always trying to make me feel less than whole. Because of this we do not see much of each other. Having survived a youthful life of abuse, I am very in tune with someone infringing on my personal area. I know before they know what they are doing, and what they are getting at too soon. It often grates on them like a rasp on a piece of pine. Finally, now I know what I need from my brother and I can demand from him to be treated as a whole person. It hurts to know I don't have a positive relationship with my only sibling. At least now we are aware of each other's pain, and we hope we can meet with a third party and work to resolve our differences.

By the time I was a teenager I was too big to beat. My parents then switched their tactics from physical abuse to emotional and psychological abuse. I always got a steady dose of "Why can't you be more like your brother" or "Boy, are you stupid" or "You will never amount to anything," etc. I found it very hard to be able to love my abusers. Indeed, it is a tough, tough lesson to try and learn.

Even when I was eight or nine I was often told that I would be disinherited, that I was a bad boy. I was even blamed because I was breech born. Because it was such a terribly hard birth, my mother had almost died. My father's hatred of me stems from my birth experience. I was often criticized because I "gave mother so much trouble being delivered." Life is tough when from birth; you are "it!" You never get to play hide-and-seek because life is being the seeker.

I really thought that there was something wrong with me. I had hoped that if I waited long enough my parents would accept me as a full, happy member of the family, but it wasn't to be. Because they didn't accept me I felt so guilty and angry. I was sure that the abuse I received was my fault. But in my anger I focused my losses on the gains of others and blamed them for my problems. I thought I was crazy. I even used to hurt myself thinking that I would get sympathy from my parents when they saw the injury. But I never showed them. I was too ashamed. So I would suffer my physical pain alone.

By the time I was 12, I was contemplating suicide. Due to my mental and emotional turmoil I had few friends and no close relationships that lasted more than a few weeks. Life seemed so awful that only death was or could be the reward for what I had gotten in life. As I look back now, I think it would have been less confusing and less detrimental to me if I had been put in a foster home. Instead, I ran away from home at 12, only to be returned when I was 14.

When I was 16, I found myself in a tough place, as my father was also my principal and my church rector or spiritual leader. When I revolted against it I was at odds with them all. An unholy trinity, a dark god of family, theology, and education—all cast a shadow upon me. It was at 16 that I tried to shoot myself because I was failing at my school work and I couldn't see that passing could ever be achieved. I was placed in a mental institution. That's when I dropped out of high school. I was failing and school was just more abuse to me. It was no escape. One of my vivid memories was of the times that my math teacher in junior high would put my head under the folding desktop of my desk and then slam it down on my head. It taught me to hate math.

We really need to discover another way to evaluate where our children are in school rather than having passing or failing grades. We need to see that for some children, getting a "B" is for them being at 100 percent. We also need to get away from calling some behaviors "deviant." There ought to be ways to encourage creativity in our children, even though what they create is not always to our way of thinking positive, growing, loving, etc. It is our knocking just one thing that can kill something else.

At 17 I ran away again and joined the U.S. Navy. I may have been 17 in age and 6'6" tall, but I had the emotional maturity of a ten-year-old. I soon found out that the Navy, actually the world, is a frightening place. I left the Navy when I was 21. I got a GED and went to college, but my emotional insecurity kept me from succeeding. I was drunk often. I tried to run away from life, drunk or sober. Soon I dropped out of college and went to work.

Work, too, was a bewildering experience. On the outside I looked 23 or 24, but on the inside I was still just a small lad. I even got married. I needed a mommy, however, not a wife. We had a child and I became a daddy without being able to cope on my own. At 28 I was divorced. Next, I had a nervous breakdown.

The hospital and doctors put me on Thorazine. That zonked me out for the next 12 months. I can remember lying on the floor in a rented room and staring at a naked light bulb hanging from the ceiling for what seemed like forever. I kept it on day and night.

One day it came to me that I needed to escape or I would die at 30, achieving nothing but screwing up my life. By this time, my family treated me as if I was dead. That was actually positive, however, because they were no longer directing me negatively. Prior to age 30 I cannot, nor have I been able to think of positive, loving family strengths directed toward me. Later I took a course based on the book *Iron John* and from that I learned my main sadness in life, that I had received nothing positive from my family. Realizing all of this I took the rest of my savings and bought an airline ticket to Australia.

I arrived in Sydney, and got off the plane with one suitcase and 200 U.S. dollars. I knew no one. Soon I got a job in a store but was fired shortly afterwards. Next I got a job selling business machines and I learned how to earn lots of money. But, I was drunk every night. Eventually I got remarried to an Aussie lassie but the marriage only lasted four years. Life was so frustrating to me, as I didn't know how to take control of my life. When you are down and life in general is rushing on, you know you are losing in big chunks. After that I overdosed on Thorazine and anything else I could find. I almost died before I realized that the only person who was abusing me now was me!

Life from 16 to 37 was only survival. By 37 I had been married and divorced twice. I had been in and out of hospitals for overdoses of any drug I could find; I had lots of stomach pumpings. I'd also been in lots of mental institutions for breakdowns, drug abuse (mostly alcohol), and for threatening suicide, which maybe were my calls for help. I had very few skills for survival. I was immature, poorly educated, a social misfit, a nonperson almost.

I credit three people with turning my life around; two by their personal help, Ted and Susan, and one by the book *The Guide to the Use of the Intensive Journal,* by Ira Progoff. They taught me to believe in me and slowly, with patience and tolerance they helped me to put my life on a positive course. I am still on that course!

Ted was almost the first person I met when I got to Australia. He invited me home, fed me Sunday night dinners for 13 years, and made me a member of his family. I married his eldest daughter. He was never critical or judgmental of me. He was at peace within himself. He was initially self-taught and then weekly schooled in yoga. His commitment was complete to me. When his daughter and I were divorced, he said, "I have not lost a son-in-law, I have lost a daughter!" Good for me and terrible for her!

Ted was my mentor in my search for mental peace. Ted had found his peace in life and was saved from the booze that tried to defeat him. He showed me by his example that I could turn my life around. But he never insisted I do anything but go at my own pace and in my own direction.

Susan was perhaps the second person I met in Australia. Susan had been a child prodigy, a violin virtuoso, and was concert mistress of a symphony orchestra by the time she was 21. She got married that same year and she was all set up for the "good life." Then something snapped in her head, she explained to me. She became mentally very ill. She tried, seriously tried suicide and I could still see, when I met her, the horrible long bluish scars running from her elbows to her fingers where she had sliced herself. She was divorced by her husband and sort of divorced by her mother and brother, too. She became afraid of the world and had a lot of treatment. When I met her she was staging comebacks in between her bouts of depression.

Susan got me to believe in me. I took a first step; I put my trust in her and said "lead on." She persuaded me that I was okay and that I did not need Thorazine or any other artificial substance to live. She got me sober. Drinking was very bad for me; it exacerbated my emotional loss of control. Once I was drunk I would lose everything: self-respect, self-esteem, money, property, consciousness, life itself. She was also one of the forces that got me off of my four-packs-a-day cigarette habit. She, along with Ted, introduced me to the Theosophical Society's book room in the Melbourne public library where there were a lot of self-help books, self-help group sessions, and so forth.

Susan could not help herself, however, and neither could I. So eventually she crawled underneath her mother's house and died from an overdose of barbiturates. In her death, she gave me life. I became "born again," not in the Christian sense, but in life. Susan was the catalyst to "tie together" Ted, Susan, and Ira Progoff's book.

I began journaling with a small group early in 1972. When I left Australia in the fall of 1984 I was still journaling in the group. Ira Progoff taught me that I should write down my story many, many times and in many different ways to "let go and let God."

No experience was ever so rewarding and ever so needed as was my twelve years of journaling. After those of us in the small group would write down our experiences, we would share them orally with each other. Until I was 30 I had had no one to talk with. Learning to talk about my problems was one of the big learning experiences of my life. By hearing the other peoples' stories I learned I was only unique in detail, not in experiences.

I began as a social misfit and found peace, happiness, love, and a whole large group of serendipitous values. For instance, in a dream learning experience I learned to "see" my way through reoccurring nightmares. I learned that my dreams had good or positive endings when I saw them through. The values were that they did not reoccur and I was finally able to lose my fear of darkness.

Because I could write things down and "let go," I got control of my life. I then went back to college and graduated in Australia. College was helpful. I majored in urban studies which formally filled in great blank spaces in my social-theoretical understanding. I've always been tenacious. When I learned to hold onto positive events, I "instantly" realized what benefits I could reap. I found I had an inquiring mind with sound reasoning ability, after I finally got all that emotional stuff into an order that I could prioritize, look at, understand, research, etc. In my employment, too, I began to excel. Now my job and my life had direction. I was positively motivated and I was, therefore, positively rewarded. I could finally see that life was a process. That meant changes could happen if I could learn how to make changes myself.

No more smoking, drinking, self-abuse, or other self-defeating activities. The more negative areas I gave up, I refilled with positive, loving experiences. In me, I found myself, and the "myself" I found was a wonderful, caring, loving person, just itching to get life going with the "right stuff."

With the new me, I came back to the U.S.A. in the 1980s to search for the "roots" to my problems. By that time I had figured out that forgiveness is the first step in learning to love. I had forgiven my parents. When I came home from Australia they could see it. Then we could grow together. However, it was with a lot of pain that I diligently uncovered the truth from both of my parents before they died. "And the truth shall set you free," with a lot of hard work and soul-searching, etc.

Since then I have remarried. In my other two marriages I thought I would find someone to take care of me, just as a child. What a disaster for marriage. Now I have a wonderful spouse and we are in our eighth year of marriage. She, too, has helped me so much along my way. Now that my needs are less, we have found some good support groups in our church-related activities for us. We have also had a year of couples' counseling. We have had to work to achieve a growing, positive marriage. And we are still working, as well as loving, enjoying, and liking. Still it's not always easy. Because of my childhood experiences I am 100 pounds overweight. This also has a lot to do with my lack of self-esteem, something I always have had trouble with. Our sex life, too, has been affected. I am often afraid to share my love (penis) with my wife. She has to be patient with me and often be the instigator of our lovemaking.

Also, you have to remember, I dropped out of raising a family when I was 28 and didn't start again with grown-ups until I was 47. Maybe now I can avoid too many falls. But, I never wanted children because my childhood was so hard as I was growing up. I still have a daughter from my first marriage to whom I was a poor parent. I have only seen her three times, one day each, since she was four years old. I do write her a lot. She has heard some of my story, as do my present wife's children. My present wife has three children to whom I am an unwanted stepfather. Luckily, they are grown and we might make it in some meaningful relationships if we all keep working at what we have. Still, I am not sure how to treat them. I do much better with younger friends who are not family members of ours. My wife and I offer a lot of our time, when asked to do so, to help younger acquaintances get their lives together. It's sort of like pastoral counseling.

We are always glad to offer our home to numerous friends and acquaintances that are lost. We encourage talk and reading to learn self-help ways to overcome adversity. Our doors will always be open to people who stray, by their own guidance or by the guidance from others. We try to share the roads we have traveled, and, therefore, we have many close friends because of the sharing. When my troubles were "big time" no one was interested. Now that I have made my way on my own, lots of people want to help.

In our church group our friends, a lot of whom knew my parents, have found all the sides to my story very traumatizing. I have volumes of pain written down and filed away and even thrown away. However, unless it comes up in discussions with friends or family, my childhood is finally at rest and peace. It is not fully cured though. But we have consistently kept the doors to my life open. It is a tough story to tell but every telling brings new revelations and uncovers more areas to be examined. If I live long enough I know I'll get light into all the dark spaces.

Work, too, is rewarding. I have been promoted through the company's ranks from salesman to sales manager to sales and marketing manager to marketing manager. After one year of being a salesman, my employer asked if I could train people to do what I could do: winning at selling. I said yes. I feel that I am a wonderful sales person, sales trainer, and personnel manager because my feelings are open and receptive to the needs of my work associates. Four-and-a-half years ago I hired a young college grad who wanted to be a salesman in our small company (nine salesmen). Now he is the number one salesman in our company. He outsells the number two man two to one. My varied childhood-to-adulthood experiences made me receptive to this fellow's needs so we could enjoy together his experiences of learning to sell. I've now trained nine men to win at what they do, and to know that they are learning to be winners. Being with the same employer for five-and-a-half years is also a record for me.

Besides the life challenges, the work challenge, the spouse growth, and love experience, I have added new challenges to my life. Most of my childhood-related hobbies and activities I discontinued as I learned about my childhood, so now I have started gardening, working with computers, photography, writing, etc.

I don't know if what I (we) have is "the best" we can have, but I do know that it is one hell of a long way from where I was 50 years ago.

My life was 16 years of parental abuse, 16 to 19 years of self-abuse, and 19 years of transition into loving, learning, and continuing.

I'll never lose, fully, the painful start I got in life, but now it is tempered with many more positive experiences. Life is a process. As long as I am proceeding in life then I will find issues to resolve. The more I uncover, the more I find to discover. I have found in men's groups that those men who started life with a loving, caring family really got an accelerated start compared to mine. But where I am now is very similar to where they are now. From my childhood I have dealt with some of the negatives and learned their positive benefits. I feel I have actualized on more areas than I have areas to go. When I see others less fortunate than I am I know that "there but by the grace of God go I." I am truly a lucky person because I learned as an adult I can control some of the luck I get. I can see in my mind's eye coming to full wholeness one of these days.

Because I have fallen to the pits of life and then clawed my way up to where I am now, I have a certain perspective which says the lows I face will never be as low as they once were. And the highs will soar beyond imaginable previous highs. I have a positive slope in life. I have learned that I have within me all the ingredients for love, success, goodness, health, well-being, etc., and I am in a process to learn to apply myself to achieve a certain measure of those benefits. With tolerance and patience the world awaits my entrance. With tenacity and perseverance I will succeed. I have started my trek. Along the way there has been pain but also triumph. The further I travel the better I can travel. The hill becomes a gentle slope. I can see the light. I can see a whole lot of things yet to do. But, I'm a late bloomer and I've just gotten underway. So look out, 'cause here I come!!!

Chapter 8

It Made Me a Better Person

One of the participants wrote a short story about her life and how, as an adult, she became a wise person, capable of helping others:

> A young girl is in a cave and is attacked repeatedly by birds and wild animals. She loses much of her ability to speak, hear, see, and move and is in constant pain. A prince comes and takes her away. He has magical butterflies that heal her by beating their wings near her. A bad winter comes and the butterflies die, but more come with the spring and they are even more beautiful and magical.

> Because the girl has been hurt, and then healed, she can help other people to find the magic butterflies. She marries the prince and her children know where to find the butterflies when they need them. Some of her children help tend the butterflies. The girl becomes a wise old woman.

One of the amazing findings in this study was that even though participants lived through "hell," 73 percent felt they were better people today because of what they experienced. The majority said their experiences affected their job or career choices, and many ended up in helping careers. The dark thread affected every aspect of their lives, and most viewed the experience as providing them with qualities that contributed to their abilities to be caring and loving people. The four peoples' stories in this chapter illustrate the positive effects the childhood trauma ultimately had on their lives.

The first story is about a German, Christian woman who, as a child, lived through war-torn Nazi Germany. The physical injuries resulting

Surviving and Transcending a Traumatic Childhood
© 2007 by The Haworth Press, Inc. All rights reserved.
doi:10.1300/5839_08

from bombings, abuse from Nazi soldiers, homelessness, and hunger all contributed to the determined, self-made person she became.

The second story is about a woman whose father drugged her and forced her into satanic cult activities. This woman's life as a child has to be one of the most severe cases of abuse in the study. As an adult, she continued to live with severe physical and psychological effects. Today, she professionally helps others who have been abused, especially those who have experienced abuse in cults. She said, "All in all, I believe it made me a better person, committed to educating and helping others."

The third story is told by a woman who spent nine years in an orphanage after her mother left her, her father, and her siblings. She became a special education teacher and believed that her childhood experience had a positive effect on her.

The final story in this chapter is of a woman who lived through beatings and being thrown down stairs. She concludes that as an adult one can create one's own family that is loving and supportive. She felt, after her childhood experiences, that she had developed the wisdom to be able to help others.

WHAT WAS, WAS, IT CANNOT BE CHANGED
WHAT IS, IS, BUT CAN BE CHANGED
WHAT COMES, COMES, BE ON THE OFFENSIVE

Growing up in war-torn Germany was, indeed, a difficult beginning for this sixty-two-year-old German woman. Not being a member of the Nazi Party made life for her and her family very challenging. Her story is a lesson in history that we should never forget:

The war which started in 1939 was very much a part of my everyday life as a child. There was constant bombing night after night, being shot at by airplanes, the loss of a number of friends and relatives, and not knowing what was going to happen next made growing up fast a necessity.

My father was a professional soldier until 1933. We lived on the base until he refused to take the Hitler oath. After war was declared he was sent over to the Russian front because our family had refused to join the Nazi Party. My only sibling, my brother, joined the army at 16. My mother was forced to work, as all women had to, leaving me on my own. Even in school I was on my own because everyone knew that we were not Nazis. But I am so glad that my mother decided to keep us all together during the war. At that time many children were sent to safe camps in other parts of the countryside. I would have really been alone then. At least we had each other.

I remember many scary times when I was young. I remember going to church on Sunday while the Hitler Youth meetings were being held at the same time. After Mass I would have to walk a row of uniformed girls and leaders, while each one of them would spit in my face. Another memory was about the time mother and I were awakened in the middle of the night by the Gestapo, the German FBI, who accused us of signaling the enemy with lights during a blackout.

A really scary instance was when my mother was very ill and bombs started falling. When I realized that I couldn't carry her down three flights of stairs I nearly went crazy with fear. But we stayed together, holding one another out of love for each other. Another time I seemed to have a real problem during an air-raid. We had had to go to the bomb shelter. Once I was there I refused to leave, I refused help and food. After the air warden pointed a gun at me to get me out, I finally realized that nothing else would help, so I marched out never to set foot in there again. Also, there was a time I had to identify our next door neighbors' bodies after a bomb had gone straight through their four-story house 10 days before. Some of them I knew only by pieces of jewelry or clothing or other parts of them, as their faces were gone. Go away, hell of a war!

In 1942 I was hurt during a bombing raid. Both of my knees were injured. There were no doctors except military ones. So after going to doctor after doctor during and after the war, I was finally accepted for three surgeries in 1952 and 1953. My legs hurt so much I wished I had none. I was warned that I might never walk again. I did, however, with therapy and determination. I was raised in an atmosphere of "do your best and then more, never say I can't!"

In the meantime, I was also a single mother. My fiancé decided to immigrate to Australia instead of marrying me. My son was born in 1949 and I raised him with the help of my parents. Another saying my parents had was, "You cooked the soup and you eat it, but if it is too hot, we will help you blow and cool it. But, you still eat it!" I was then forced to get part-time work while wearing braces on both of my knees. My parents helped with me and my son by letting me live at home, but I paid my own expenses. If something special came up that I wanted, I sacrificed for it. Like, I would walk to work a half hour on my bad knees to be able to get a coat, which was more than I could manage to pay for otherwise.

Everyone had to depend on themselves for survival. It was self-preservation or die. Mothers forgot children and children forgot mothers. People behaved like animals. Once, I saw a baby in a carriage being trampled to death by a bunch of SS officers who wanted to get into a bunker first after the air-raid siren went off.

Discrimination against people makes me angry. I learned this long before I saw a black person or came to America and actually encountered it. Because I didn't belong to the Nazi Party I felt discrimination as a child while I was in Germany. There were many who believed in the Nazi system probably out of fear or brainwashing, or because they were trying for a better position. After I came to America I felt discrimination as an adult. Because I was German, people, even my in-laws, assumed I was a Nazi. I was called names by ignorant people who really didn't know me personally. No one knew that there were two kinds of Germans: those for and those against Hitler. It would have been nice to have found someone who I could tell everything to, but perhaps putting it in writing would have helped, too.

My dad's secretary was part Jewish. We didn't know this until it was required to prove that you were Aryan or non-Jewish in order to hold a job with the city or government. After it was found out, my dad had to fire this man. We could have no contact with him after that. He later just vanished.

I can still vividly recall the people cheering and laughing as we were forced to watch as Jewish houses were attacked with clubs, axes, etc. Everything was smashed: doors, windows, and the crystal chandeliers which hung in every foyer of Jewish apartment houses. Furniture was most often thrown out windows, but sometimes it got out of hand and people got thrown off balconies. Screaming children got stomped on with booted feet from the Storm troopers, the brown-uniformed Nazis. Afterwards, all was set on fire, the whole Jewish section of town burned as it was surrounded by troopers so the fire department could not come in.

Life was hard for everyone. During the bombing most of our town was destroyed. Relatives lost everything two to three times. Once we dug out by hand after hours in the rubble, our own apartment had only one inside wall left. There was cooking gas for one hour per day. We burned books, and salvaged wood for heat. I can remember waking up with ice formed on my blanket because there was no glass in the windows in the room. There was no electricity most days but we could get some food with ration stamps if available. For three weeks in the bomb shelter we had only crackers with butterfat, coconut fat and fish margarine, and wine.

Some people discovered wine cellars after a bombing, and the wine ran in the gutters after looting. We were so hungry that once we walked for four to five hours to try and trade mother's damask table-cloth for food from farmers. I remember that we begged for potatoes and were chased off one place by the dogs. I sneaked away as mother collapsed on the side of the road, and I did something for the first and only time in my life: I stole potatoes by digging them up out of a field.

I really believe that I survived because of my family's strong up-bringing of self-preserve, a will to do our best and then push for more, and not to blame others for failures. I have no bitter feelings for any-one involved in the war for the wrongdoings that were done. Every-one believed that he or she was right and they were entitled to those beliefs. Good or bad, they had to live with them. Everyone went through this emotional event. I made the transition from wartime to peace fairly well by keeping an open mind and by always trying to look on the good side, as the next person may be worse off. My par-ents and friends were also helpful to me, as they would listen to me when the burden got too much. I found, once or twice, that it really helped to open up to others.

My religious beliefs didn't falter during the war as relatives got killed or dad didn't get to come home on leave. It made me under-stand that God sometimes shows a bad thing to make you see the good better. Prayers helped me through tough times, but first of all I believed in myself. Through prayer one does not feel alone. Even if someone does not believe in God, there are always feelings of some-thing more powerful than oneself. One doesn't have to go to a church to pray, either. You can do it anywhere.

School is important. One can never learn too much. Going to school during the war was difficult, as schools were being destroyed and you had to keep changing classes and teachers often. But still, education and making passing grades were important. I finished school during the war and afterwards got my license for teaching nursery school and for being a governess. As a governess or nanny I would talk to children from the first day on and I would listen to them. Even with adults you should try to understand their feelings and try to make them open up without making any judgments for or against them. With children, I would also read to them and let them tell of their troubles with drawings or stories. I feel you should educate children about life and death by showing them newborns and dead persons, as there is always a beginning and an end.

When I couldn't get a job in my field, I simply trained for another, including working as a dishwasher or ward at a U.S. military hospital. After immigrating to America, the job I found there helped me to become a more adjusted person. I was trusted completely to raise three children and to run a household, which included overseeing the duties of the maid and the gardener, etc., even when my employers were abroad. My trust in people grew stronger as this employer, who was a millionaire, included both me and my son in their family. We are still in touch with each other today.

Without the war I wouldn't need to have artificial knees and I wouldn't have lost family and friends. My whole life would have been different, I am sure. I could have been a different person, but maybe a bad one. What was, was, it cannot be changed. What is, is, but can be changed. What comes, comes, be on the offensive. I have achieved most things I wanted up 'til now. The disadvantages of age will not stop me. It may slow me down, but I will keep going as long as I can. I think that I also adjusted well because I never lost my sense of humor, and I am able to get along with most people. I try to accept people the way they are. No one is perfect and I will not hesitate to tell a person that, but there are a lot of decent, good people out there. I forgive but won't forget if someone hurts me too deep.

I worked for 11 years in a nursing home and have done lots of volunteer work and I have learned to be patient and understanding. I really do believe that I am a 99 percent happy and well-adjusted woman. I try everything once, and some things twice. Sometimes

I win and sometimes I lose but, to me, life is what I make it and I refuse to give up.

It still hurts that I had to leave my home in Germany, and it hurts to think that it could have been different. It helps to read letters and see the news about home. Hearing sirens, seeing guns in the wrong hands (I can and will shoot a gun without fear if I have to), seeing the swastika, uniforms at demonstrations, some TV programs, and any type of war still causes me pain.

I have found that if I block out the pain of the past instead of reliving it over and over, it still surfaces. Actually, I hardly think about my past at all anymore, but I have had nightmares where I hear bombs whistling through the air and I feel the ground shaking as they explode and I see the buildings shake and dead people all around. It helped me to be able to talk about it with others. I know some who have not talked about these things. One friend from Germany in particular has had three breakdowns which I think comes from repressed feelings.

I look forward to letting go of the past someday, but I find it very scary to see the new Neo-Nazi Party on TV. I fear a new uprising from these young people who were not born and don't know the old Nazi party as it existed then. It awakened more memories in me, including disgust, and sends me into turmoil.

In 1959 I married and am proud to say that I am still happily married today to the same man. However, as my husband has emphysema and congestive heart failure I am doing home health care for him. We have two adult children that I may have been a little too strict with at times, but each one turned out good. My oldest one completed 21 years in the Air Force. I will help other people if I am asked. Otherwise, I don't interfere with anyone else's life, not even my own children's. We did our best to raise them. If they mess their life up, they have to make good. There is always an open door to come home to, however.

When they asked me about my childhood I showed them pictures and answered their questions, without too many details. When they couldn't have one thing or another, I told them that it would not be a disadvantage to them. I survived without having any teenage years at all. One cannot predict your destiny in the world, you can only make your own life good or bad.

Accept, forgive, and forget as much as possible is the philosophy I live by. My advice to myself and to others is don't give up, look forward not back, but do not forget the good or the bad. Make do with what you have and always believe in yourself. I had a good relationship with my family. They always told me to be a good person and never give up, to read a lot, to stay with reality, and to be myself. Also, people should not ignore things just because it's not near to where you are. Be on top and do not let other people put you down.

I can laugh at myself, my mistakes and can, if necessary, shrug off criticism. But I am a very outspoken person. I voice my opinion in front of organizations, clubs, legislators, and I don't trust political promises at all. Also, I get into arguments if some arrogant person dubs me as a German who did nothing to prevent the Holocaust. I often get asked why I didn't do something to prevent it from happening. I tell them what it was like. I say speak up now, not after everything is over. And don't forget that law and order means it is for everyone. Stand up for your rights.

All of us, one time or another, hit a low time in life. I did, but I laugh at my own faults and go and close the door and have a cry if things get too tough. No one wants your trouble. Everyone has some of their own. I despise persons who say, "I can't," without trying. I never quit pushing myself to achieve more, to get as much out of life as possible. I stand up to anything or anybody and I argue my point if I feel I am in the right. Sometimes I do put my foot in my mouth, but usually I either apologize, even if it's hard to admit, or stand by my action. I believe in equal rights so I voice my opinion, right or wrong.

I grew up in a country terrorized by a dictatorship. It taught me to think for myself. When I was only five or six years old I was asked by a women's group, that my mother was required to belong to, to give flowers to Adolf Hitler in a welcoming ceremony. I refused. "Hard head" I was called then, and still am today. But my determination made me what I am, and sees me through life. I am self-made and what I have I earned by working for it alone and side-by-side with my family and my husband. I will not back away from tasks. I try!

FROM ANGEL CHILD TO THE DEVIL'S CHILD BY THE AGE OF SIX

Fourteen years of emotional and physical abuse might seem like almost too much for anyone to overcome, but this European American woman now forty-one years of age feels that she has survived and transcended her traumatic childhood:

Shortly after I turned four I became gravely ill with a multitude of problems, including kidney disease and meningitis, and I was hospitalized off and on for about two years. During that time, my mother told me later, my parents were called to the hospital three or four times to say good-bye to me because I wasn't supposed to make it through the night. Well, I did, but that is when the problems began.

When I finally got well enough to come home from the hospital my mother told me that I used to be the "angel child," but while I was in the hospital the devil took me over. That is when the abuse began. It was mostly verbal to start with, but the first physical abuse I remember was the day I got home from the hospital. I was told that I wasn't supposed to get out of bed, and as I couldn't walk at all I kept calling for my mother to come and help me. I remember feeling very nauseous. Well, she never did come and I knew that she must have heard me because our house was very small, so I had no choice but to throw up all over myself and everything else. Then she came, yelling and hitting me. Finally, she pulled me out of bed and threw me onto the floor and told me to clean up my mess. I couldn't even stand up, so I had to crawl, dragging the dirty sheets and everything else I'd dirtied to the bathroom so I could clean them up. I still remember her cursing at me and yelling that she wished her angel hadn't died in the hospital.

Maybe if my mother would have gotten counseling to help her control her temper and her depression all this wouldn't have happened. But, my parents were not happily married and as I try to make sense of it all now, I think that my mother was so miserable that the only way she could handle her misery was to take it out on me. When my parents got along with each other things were much better for me. I don't think I ever was punished when they were happy.

My father must have known what was happening because he was home at times, but he was so very busy he pretty much left us alone. Anyway, he never got her to stop and he swears now that he never knew about it. He did drink, however, and he could be very cruel to my mother when he yelled at her. Of course, after he would leave the house I'd get "treated." I was sure I deserved my "treatments," after all I was the "devil's child."

Besides my mom being miserable in an unhappy marriage, I think that another reason she picked on me was that I was the only daughter that looked like her. I could be her clone. I remember seeing a picture of her when she was about ten years of age. I thought it was me dressed in "funny clothes," and couldn't figure out how this picture was taken without my remembering it. That's when I really got scared, I felt I was doomed to become my mother.

My family was a very strict Norwegian, Lutheran family. We went to church, Sunday school, fellowship, and choir. I knew that there was a God and I was terrified of Him because I was a fallen angel. I was so sure that no one loved me that at times I wanted to die. I remember getting a book on Egypt and seeing the Pharaoh's mummy, and then trying to replicate that picture by lying in my bed at night like the dead Pharaoh. My hands were crossed across my chest, waiting to die. Mother caught me doing this and said I was crazy. In actuality, I knew that I couldn't kill myself because Satan would get my soul and I'd be damned in hell for all eternity. So you see, even if there had been someone to talk to, I was too ashamed to tell anyone, for I made it happen by being the devil's child and I deserved my punishment.

Still, I reasoned that if I injured myself maybe mother wouldn't hurt me anymore. I remember trying to break my feet by dropping bricks on them. Surely, if I had a cast on she would leave me alone. I didn't succeed in breaking my feet, although I did try. But, I stopped because I became too afraid of what she would say when I made up a reason for how it happened. I was convinced that she would know when I lied.

Confirming my feelings of self-degradation even more, I remember once seeing the lady next door watching through the window while my mother beat me. All the lady did was close her window and pull the blind. No one helped me, I didn't deserve it.

I did go to school and I had friends. My best friend today is a woman I met in second grade. We started our friendship by walking to school together. But neither she nor the rest of my friends could ever come to my house. The closest I remember ever coming to mentioning anything about what was happening to me was when I asked a friend in the sixth grade if she had ever been spanked. She told me that she hadn't been spanked since kindergarten. I lied and said, "Me neither."

I was not an only child. I am the second of three daughters, but neither of my sisters were ever punished beyond the "norm" of the '50s and '60s. In my family we were categorized. My older sister was the smart one, my younger sister was the pretty one, and I was the bad, dumb one. Oh, they got spanked and slapped, but I was the only one thrown down stairs or locked in the basement and told that she hoped that the spiders would eat me up. Once I was locked in the basement, I was not permitted to have the light on, to have food, bed, or blankets and I was left there all night. I would cry and scream at first, but no one could help me. I honestly don't know if anyone ever tried. To this day I am terrified of dark, close places, and of spiders. I'm working on overcoming these fears.

Another "treatment" I received was to be beaten with balloon sticks because they left no broken bones and were very effective in their results. There was a kind of ritual to this treatment: First, I would have to go to the spare bedroom and take off all my clothes. Then I would have to wait, for sometimes a very long time it seemed, until my mother had decided that I had thought about my most recent "crime" long enough. Then, she would come in and whip me with the balloon sticks. When she started doing this treatment, before the balloon sticks, she used her hand. But it must have hurt her too much, because then she started using a piece of driftwood that she had found down at the lake. It left too much visible evidence though, as I couldn't hold my hands away while I was getting hit. Then, as luck would have it, my grandmother came by with balloons for us girls, balloons on long, hard, twisted, plastic sticks. That's when mom discovered that these plastic sticks could have another use. They were not permanently disfiguring, but were very effective disciplinary tools. Besides stinging, they made a hideous whistling sound as they flew through the air and an awful sound as they connected with my body. Still, I was only hit in places that would be covered with clothing so no one would see the marks.

My older sister, by two-and-a-half years, used to come into the spare bedroom with me before mother would begin her whipping. She would promise that this time she was going to tell mom to hit her and not me. I used to believe her, but each time as my mom was coming in she would run and hide in the closet and scream along with me. I know now that Mary's trying to take my punishment would have only gotten us both hurt. Somehow I think I was better able to overcome this than Mary was, because my punishment was over when mom stopped abusing me. But Mary has felt guilty all of her life for not helping me. Finally, just last November, she and I had a most wonderful talk in which we discussed all that had happened. I think now she has finally released the guilt. We both ended up crying and it has brought us closer together.

My little sister, Jenny, was "my baby." I loved her and wanted to make sure that she didn't get "treatments," so I protected her. I didn't want anyone to ever harm her. When I look at both of my sisters today, I see that I am the happiest, most successful of the three of us. I have worked hard to overcome my childhood, but it had to get worse, much worse, before I was able to get to where I am today.

As I got older, the punishments got more severe. Sometimes she would rip off my clothes or try to push me out of the third-floor window. The worst part of all this was that it wasn't consistent punishment. There were times when I could get away with certain things and other times when I would get punished for doing nothing at all. I remember getting hit for things my little sister did, because I must have taught her how to do it.

Finally, at 20 I escaped by marrying a man I was not in love with. Even though he was verbally abusive and was tending more and more to be physically abusive before I took my son and left him, I still believe that my marriage saved my life. I am sure that my mother would have killed me if I wouldn't have left home.

When I was about to get my divorce about ten years ago, my husband and I went into family counseling. One of the things that the counselor asked about was happy times in our childhoods with our mothers. That really threw me. I couldn't think of or remember a thing. I literally got sick and had to leave. I discovered that I had repressed everything about my traumatic childhood from the age of 20, when I got married, until the age of 30. Through counseling I soon realized that I had married to get out of the house with my life, not because I was in love.

I continued on with the counselor for the next year or so after divorcing my husband. My therapist helped me, but it took my own "death" for me to really overcome my childhood. You see, I became so depressed when I was dredging all of this up, because I felt certain that I was doomed to become my mother. And as I didn't want to hurt my son, even though I had never laid a hand on him or spanked him or was ever verbally abusive to him, I was sure that I would beat him eventually. So I tried to starve myself. I truly wanted to die, but I didn't want it to look like suicide so I pretended to not be able to eat. I am five foot seven and at one point I got down to 87 pounds. I spent a lot of time having fluids and nutrients forced into me in the hospital.

You will probably think I am crazy, but shortly after I left the hospital, which turned out to be for the last time, I went back to my starvation diet. At one point, I remember clearly getting up out of bed and taking a few steps and then fainting. It was then that I saw my body below me, for I seemed to be rising up into the air above my body, above my house and then above my city. I believe I "died." I was next in a tunnel "going to the light." I was so happy and peaceful, I wanted to stay. But, I was sent back and told that it wasn't my time yet. More happened but that's another story. That's when my life really turned around. I began eating again and really wanted to live again. At last my therapy really made sense. Now you're sure I'm crazy, right? I'm not.

Now I can share with others my painful experiences if I need to, but I never could have at first. My son was there while I was reliving all of the memories. He knew I was in pain, but we went through it together. I had him go through counseling and a support group at school to help him. I know that I am less critical and more accepting, and more supportive of my son's special talents than I would have been otherwise. I am certain of this. Also, I was able to finally admit what had happened to me to my best friend from the second grade. After I shared my childhood trauma with her, we cried together.

I tried approaching my mother about all of this, but she denies everything. It never happened. We have no contact. She still thinks I'm crazy, so my little sister says, and I'm okay with that. My father and I are very close now. He has apologized to me, and I know he loves me. I have forgiven my parents, but it was imperative for the healing process that I forgive myself, also, for not fighting back. Now I know that I am a worthwhile, loving, caring human being. I have goodness inside of me and I try to help spread joy wherever I go.

Once in awhile there are still some unresolved issues that rise up, but I am able to handle them. "Flashbacks" do happen, too, and they make me feel that I am suddenly back to being a child once again, and feeling very scared and helpless. Many things can trigger them: movies, books, mothers in the grocery store yelling at their kids, and even my own reflection in the mirror. I still look like my mother. Nightmares also occur from time to time. In them I am being chased and know I am going to be killed. I always give up; then I wake up. But now, too, I have positive dreams about my helping many people who need help, or sometimes I dream of my mother begging for my forgiveness.

Today, I'm still alive and thriving. It still hurts that no one was there for me; no one cared enough to make my mother stop. But, I now believe that life is wonderful. Not perfect, but worth living. I've found that if your birth family isn't healthy, you can create your own "real" family with people who support and love you.

These experiences have strengthened me and given me the wisdom to help others who are going through what I have. There's nothing like having "been there." I really enjoy helping others in my two jobs as an administrative assistant and a crisis counselor, although I work 65 to 75 hours a week. I am also an ordained minister, a recent accomplishment. Back then it would have been the last thing I would have considered, but I have made my peace with God and know that God is loving and not hateful. I also have many friends now. It's great! I can have them in my home any time I want.

My advice to others to help a child through an emotionally stressful time would be to accentuate the good in the child and listen even if the child says nothing. Schools, too, should do their best to make each child feel special and valued. If a teacher went out of her or his way to give me positive attention, there was nothing I wouldn't do for them. To help an adult who has gone through an emotionally stressful childhood I would say listen, listen, listen, and understand that pretending it is over doesn't really make it over. It must be released or it festers and causes problems in other areas.

Truthfully, I can now say that I look to a future of excitement and challenges. I am not the devil's daughter. I am basically good, and I love being alive.

I HAVE SEEN THE DARK SIDE OF PEOPLE;
I AM EVEN MORE DETERMINED
TO SEEK THE LIGHT

The following story is perhaps the most controversial story appearing in this book. Some readers might ask, "Is this story really true? What actually happened in her life?" We have no way of knowing for certain the veracity of the story, which tells of a woman whose early years were filled with emotional, physical, and sexual abuse by her father, other relatives, and members of a satanic cult. We include her story because it is remarkable how far she believes she has come in transcending her past:

My earliest memory of being sexually abused was when I was in diapers and preverbal. My father was my first and most frequent perpetrator. His twin sister and their father also sexually abused me. By the age of five my father was orally raping me. By age eight, he was vaginally raping me. The abuse began with a velvet glove, so to speak, but by age nine, that was abandoned for other methods not so tender. Even though my father increased the frequency of his visits to two to three times a week, his abuse became so regular and repetitive that I became very good at dissociating myself with what was happening to me. My father then escalated the abuse. He became angrier and more sadistic. His need for power and dominance increased and he added random physical abuse to the sexual and emotional abuse he'd been trying. This was much more traumatic for me at the time and much harder from which to dissociate myself.

I have one memory of oral rape when I was about six where my mother came home and found us. She said in a very sorry voice, "Oh, Tom, I thought you stopped that a long time ago." He ignored her until he came, then walked out. She stroked my forehead and said, "I'm sorry." My mother doesn't remember this, but she does remember seeing my father touching my breasts at age 11. She took action then and his response was to say that he was teaching me about my body. Then he cried and said he'd never do it again. I don't remember this. Of course, he was an expert manipulator.

When I was about 7, I found out my father was also abusing my brother. I wanted to tell my mother but was unable to. When I was 9 or 10, I saw my father rape my sister for what I believe was the first and only time. I was terrified that he was hurting her because she screamed the entire time, whereas my brother and I dissociated. I think now that her screaming saved her from further abuse. He never physically abused her, as he did my brother and me. When he raped her I got the butcher knife to stop him, but then I froze and was unable to help her. I have always felt very guilty about that. Now I thank God that I could not kill, it would have started me on the path to evil.

By age 11, he was sadistically raping me and beating me in the stomach. He also would close his hands around my throat until I would pass out. This is when I started to hate him, even while I loved him. Previously, I accepted his blaming me for the abuse; he had to do it because I was bad, although I was never sure what I'd done.

Also at this time he began experimenting with ritual abuse in the basement, under the guise of developing film in the laundry room. He engaged my brother and me in pseudosatanic rituals. He would use my brother as an altar boy, the ironing board as an altar, and he would tie me onto it. He wore his college robes to play the part of the priest. As he recited the Creed he inserted knives into my vagina saying he was getting the devil out of me. Although I bled after this my brother and I never told or spoke about it.

About the time I was 12, my father began surreptitiously taking me out of the house before midnight. He'd take me to a nearby woods where a group of women dressed in white or black gowns had a special site in a circle of trees. I named them "the witch ladies" because they chanted about the devil and evil and good. I never heard them refer to themselves by any group name. The women and my father would use me in different rituals, most of it was sexual and physical torture. They built fires and had an altar, a wooden table-like structure.

Once they tethered me to a stake in the ground by my wrist and gave me a drug which caused me to hallucinate and I became frenzied. Whether it was from the drug or the group sex acted on me, I don't know. Another time, they tied me to a cross and laid it on the burning embers of their fire. I thought I'd burn to death but, as usual, they were just scaring me and took me off before any serious burning took place. This episode took place on Good Friday and they chanted for me to renounce Christ, as he was now dead.

These episodes had always taken place during the night, but one time my father took me to the woods during the day. It seemed that no one was there until we came upon an open grave dug in the ground. My father looked in and appeared horrified to see Zelda, the main witch lady lying dead in it. He then pushed me forward so that I could see. Her face was ghostly white. Suddenly, my father pushed me into the grave with her. As I fell on her, she sat up screaming and then she started laughing hysterically, my father finally joining in.

After six months or so of the witch ladies, my father began taking me to the devil people, again my name for them. All of the witch ladies were there as well as a larger group of men. The men wore black robes and hoods. The women wore white robes and hoods here, although they didn't wear hoods in their own place. Usually we went to a large barn down a long dirt road. It had been customized for their purposes.

The first time my father took me I saw a goat and an altar like the witch ladies had, and a smaller alter with a chalice, and black and purple candles. In a corner was a fire. The witch ladies were standing in a circle chanting next to the larger altar. I remember that the altar was bloody and that my father picked me up and held me over the witch ladies' shoulders so that I could see what they were gathered around. There was a bloody pile of limbs. They appeared to be small human limbs. Next, a young woman came in who was not one of the witch ladies. She was holding a child, maybe 13 or 14 months old. They undressed the toddler and put him on the altar. Then the biggest man there, who I later came to call "the Boss," as it soon became clear that he was the leader, hacked the baby into pieces with a cleaver. The baby didn't make a sound until the first chop. I think it was drugged. Then it screamed for a little while until it was dead. Next, they threw the limbs over the heads of the witch ladies into the existing pile of remains, all the while continuing with their chanting.

At some point I screamed and ran out the door. My father followed me, as the Boss yelled at him to stop me and shut me up before the police heard. I was able to elude him for about 20 feet, but the Boss had joined in the chase and he caught up with me and grabbed me. As I struggled to get away I knocked his hood partially off. I rarely saw people's faces when I was with the devil people, though my father's was usually uncovered when he was torturing me. Anyway, the Boss had a goatee and dark hair and eyes. Amazingly, I had repressed this until two years ago. Then, when I finally remembered it, I met with the state police and their artist to recreate a sketch of this man. I didn't think that I could, but with the artist's talent and experience we came up with a drawing which, when completed, scared me as much as the man did when I was actually living these experiences.

My father took me regularly to the devil people's gatherings in that barn or at another site in the woods. I don't want to relate every episode I remember, however, I will share with you the "highlights" of the worst things I saw or took part in against my will.

Usually there were other children present at these ceremonies. One time they had me and two other girls about my age tied up in a row on the altar. It was like a crazy assembly line. We were of course naked as usual, but this time the devil people walked down the row of us and beat us with bats. I had long since learned to be quiet and to dissociate as best I could from the pain. But one girl screamed and so they beat her harder until she was dead, or so I thought. I was never quite sure when death was real because they simulated it often. But, 30 days later I found out that she had died because they took me and the other remaining girl into the woods site and dug up the dead girl's grave and had a ceremony.

The day after that beating and killing, my father took me into the woods for a walk and pulled out a gun. He was always against guns before, so this surprised me. He held it very close to my temple and pulled the trigger. When I came to, my head was hurting, and my hair was burning. My father was laughing like a maniac and said, "If you talk, I'll kill you for real." He must have shot a blank and I fainted from fear and pain.

When I was almost 14 the worst ceremony took place. My father took me to a room in a basement of a house. There was an older girl lying on a cot against the far wall. A man in a white lab coat was with her. I couldn't really see what was happening as my father and Zelda were blocking my view while they were taking off my clothes and dressing me in a white robe. I had never worn one of the robes before. The man in the lab coat, a doctor I supposed, then left the room carrying something. I remember hearing the girl crying. The doctor then came back and injected my arm with something. Then Zelda and my father each took one of my arms and half dragged me into the other room. By this time I was almost catatonic from whatever it was that they'd injected me with. I could think but I couldn't move of my own volition or stand up alone. A ceremony was in progress. A purple cloth was covering a moving lump on the altar. Somehow I figured out that it was the girl in the other room's newborn baby. The Boss was there and he put a dagger in my hand and closed his hand around mine. Zelda and my father held me up by the shoulder and arm so hard I ached. After chanting something, the Boss used my hand to stab the baby under the cloth until it didn't move anymore. Then we cut out its tiny heart and everyone ate a small piece of it. The whole time I chanted silently in my head over and over, "This is not right, God does not like us to kill little babies."

The next day I awoke to find that I remembered it all vividly. Usually I was able to repress what I'd been through. I went through the day hating myself and wanting to die more than I ever had. That evening when my father came home I cornered him in the dark hallway and whispered, "I am not ever going back there." He said, "They'll kill you if you don't." Actually, I think he was more worried about them killing him than me. As I had really thought this out, my determination showed in my voice. "I'm not going back," I repeated. "I'll tell if you make me and I won't even care if they kill me. I won't ever kill again."

He must have believed me. In a few months we left the country for a year, and he didn't take me back before we left or when we returned. I got my period about a month before we left, and I thanked God that I hadn't gotten it sooner. I knew that they would have made me pregnant so they could take my baby away as they did that other girl's.

When we were out of the country my father left me alone for the most part. Of course, he had no real opportunity as there were two of us to a bedroom in our apartment. When we returned he began to rape me anally so he wouldn't get me pregnant. His physical violence continued to grow.

When I had finished high school, I left home for college, but it was in the same town where my father worked. However, he did finally let me live in a dorm on my own. My mother made him, after much fighting with him over this issue. When I saw him in downtown he would always treat me like a lover in front of other people, his associates, and my friends. People made comments which made me uncomfortable, but I couldn't quite pinpoint why I felt so uncomfortable about these encounters. After all, this was innocuous compared to the rest of my childhood.

I repressed all of the abuse until I was 27. No one knew what I had gone through except my brother, because he went through a lot of it, too. We both recognized the threat to our lives, however, if we talked, so we didn't talk, not even to each other. My sister learned early on that if she made herself invisible she wouldn't be bothered so she was no help to me at all. My mother was trained to be a good meek wife and not to question her husband. She, of course, was emotionally battered herself.

But, others did help me, though unknowingly. My grandmother would try and keep me out of my father's way whenever she could, ever since an experience when I was a crying infant which I'll tell you about a little later. And, my best friend would let me come often to her house. So, these were both escapes from home for me, as was school. My friend was also so good for me as she would match my mood, if I was depressed. She allowed me quiet time to myself. Once she and her father even took me canoeing and camping for a weekend. I treasure that memory still because he made me feel special just by being and doing things like an appropriate father.

Another good escape for me was reading. I loved to read and I found it to be such a useful escape that I read voraciously. Then there was always school work, I was good in school. I even got noticed by teachers for my good work. Another area of school I excelled in was in acting. I loved to act in plays. It, too, was an escape like reading. I could be another person and my acting teachers were special to me. Today, I still love to read and to go to the theater. I am also very good at problem solving and reaching people.

Although school got me away from my father it wasn't always the safe haven I hoped it would be. I did feel safe in elementary and high school, but in junior high I was teased and picked on often. Many classmates were very mean to me, so I didn't feel safe there. Their behavior really hurt and made me feel more lonely. Even though I didn't dare talk to anyone about my life, I did try to talk to the junior high guidance counselor about my problems at school. I would go into his office and cry that everyone hated me. He never really tried to help me with the school situation, but even if he had, I'm not so sure that I would have ever said more.

By the age of 11, or 12, I was aware that my father's behavior was wrong and that the cult was immoral. That knowledge, based on watching good people and reading the Bible, helped me to feel above them. I would constantly tell myself that they can do what they want with my body, but they can't touch my soul. My soul belongs to God. I saw God as all controlling and all powerful when I was young. Now I see man as having free will and God not liking it, but not reneging on that arrangement.

I did pray to God during my childhood, to try and make them stop hurting me. I wondered why God didn't help. Even so, my baptism as an infant into the church and reminders of our faith helped me to resist the brainwashing, the trauma, confusion, and the emotional battering done to me by my father and the cult. I really needed to reassure myself that good conquers evil. So, although I received no religious tutelage from my parents, I asked for and received a Bible in junior high. I was not brought to church, however, except by my grandparents on holidays. They and my godparents were very helpful to me in an unaware sort of way, as they helped me to keep my faith in my religion.

As an adult, my spiritual education had to be renewed, as it had been so skewed by the cult and by my father during the incest. Obviously, I had to unlearn things that I was told, and relearn new ways of looking at religion. The Satanists turn everything Christian around to the opposite, so it was very hard to go to church for awhile and see icons of Christ crucified, see the candles, hear the priest chant and to see the priest's robes, and to take communion.

I survived by dissociating, repressing, and minimizing. At 31 years of age I was diagnosed as having a dissociate disorder. Through hypnosis work we found three parts of me, Artemis, Body, and Baby.

Artemis was the decision maker and the only cognitive one. She saved my life by rationalizing, though in a very warped way, and dissociating for me when I couldn't. She also helped me to keep my mouth shut and generally to be dutiful in spite of her very strong will. Artemis decided what the rules of each game were and made sure I followed them. This was no mean feat, as my father's greatest power was that of causing confusion. Black was white and white was black until you figured it out, and then he'd change the rules again.

Also, Artemis decided when I would remember something in therapy, until I got stronger than her.

Body took all of the physical pain and abuse in silence and allowed me to go about my daily life able to hide my physical injuries. Unfortunately, as I remembered more, Body let go of the hidden pain and I began to have serious illness after serious illness. I had to have four surgeries in two-and-a-half years that were all medically diagnosed as being caused by the trauma done to my body as a child. Three of the surgeries were abdominal. At one point, I almost died from a bowel obstruction and was in the hospital for three weeks. My psychologist worked with me, my physicians, and a massage therapist to unravel the mystery of which pains were stress related, without a physical diagnosis, and which had a current medical cause.

Baby was the pure part of me, untouched by all of the evil. Artemis and Body would fight over who would hold and protect Baby. The truth was that Baby didn't need protecting, though we could never convince Artemis and Body of that. Baby, I believe, was the strongest part of me, with the most gentle spirit. Baby is why I never killed my father, why I hung onto my belief that God was stronger than the devil people, why I survived, and why I have had the strength to face it all again as an adult with repressed memories and, finally, to surpass it.

I attribute Baby mostly to my grandmother. When I was born my mother was very sick, so for the first six weeks of my life my grandmother took care of me. She would hold me much of the time, my mother says. Before she died I began telling her about the abuse and she told me the following story. When I was two weeks old the family was eating dinner and I was colicky and crying. She said that she went to pick me up but my father wouldn't allow it. He told me to shut up and of course I still cried. My grandfather tried to intervene and my father told him, "She has to learn to listen to me, if she won't listen and shut up she'll have to go in the bedroom by herself." Two weeks old! When she was able to hold me I knew that my grandmother's arms were a safe haven, and that her love was unconditional. All her efforts to keep me away from my father helped to create Baby. My godparents continued that, as did my mother, when she wasn't told not to. That's how I survived.

I transcended because of Baby and Artemis and Body's strength and stubbornness. Also because of the help of excellent psychotherapists, good friends, a superior husband, a loving mother, grandmother, and godparents, a support group, my faith, a wonderful minister, and my own sheer will power.

I can't think how my abusive childhood has not affected my life. However, of the myriad things that affected me, lack of trust, and confusion between right and wrong and good and bad seem to have been the worst factors, other than the physical effects. My body cannot heal as easily as my mind. I have a lot of health problems that have resulted from the physical trauma done to me as a child.

I knew throughout my childhood and 20s that my life was plodding along, unhappily and in pain. I suffered chronic daily migraines from the age of 21 to 28. I knew I needed to change my life and I wanted to change it. I tried without guidance or knowing the path, but, I recognized my childhood experience had been getting me involved with men who were unhealthy. I used to do whatever a man told me to do. I would always see my father's face superimposed on the man's face with whom I was having sex. I became wary of my own judgment. I had some good friends in wonderful marriages who helped me hold out for a good man instead of settling for just anyone, as I thought I would have to. So, when I finally found what I thought was a good man and fell in love with him, I was scared to commit, in case I was wrong about him. When my grandmother pronounced him a good man, like my grandfather, then I felt I was right. I didn't want anything to ruin the best thing that had ever happened to me, so I began to work on my problems. I read, I listened, and I worked.

I attended an incest support group as an adult after I was almost forced to by my psychologist, who I was seeing about a medical condition at the time. I went mainly to please him and out of fear of losing my husband whom I had just married. I really didn't think I had experienced incest, just touched sometimes. It took a few months of being pushed out the door by my husband until I went for me.

At the first meeting, I only said that I didn't think I belonged there. I sat there and rocked and cried for the rest of the time. I am not sure I would've gone back if one woman hadn't hugged me before leaving and said, "Please come back." I liked that I could bounce feelings off of other people, that I heard others describe some feelings and behaviors that I had, and I learned that I wasn't crazy for being the same. I made a few lasting friendships there, although it has always taken me awhile to get to know people and trust them because I make new friendships slowly. However, I do have very many close relationships with males and females and always have, even as a child. They are part of what got me through it all.

As a child, all of the cult experiences left me feeling crazy while I was going through them. But, I could dissociate myself into sleep and then when I awoke, I wouldn't remember the incident that had happened to me, most of the time. I guess that's what I did with the incest part of it, I dissociated and repressed it so well that I don't believe I felt crazy about that as a child.

Recalling the memories and accompanying feelings as an adult has been so overwhelming to me, especially as I realized I shouldn't repress things anymore. But, remembering and actually realizing that my father had raped me as a child, I very much felt I was going crazy, for who would do those terrible things to a small child? So I started going to therapy. Once driving to therapy, I drove my car into a tree during a snowstorm. I don't recall thinking suicidal thoughts but I believe that's just what it was. I really believed my father would kill me when I told someone about my memories. As a child I had symbolic suicidal thoughts. One time when my father was molesting me in the car and it was raining, I can remember watching the rain drops run down the windshield. I pictured myself as one of those raindrops running into the sea and then disappearing.

I have had many emotions over all that has happened to me. As a child I was told that what was done to me was my fault, so I felt guilt. When I saw children murdered and I didn't die, I felt guilt. And of course, I felt guilt when I saw my father abusing my siblings, as I felt I should have stopped him. When I try to place blame on someone for everything, I only blame those people who perpetrated me. They chose to hurt me and I still feel they are to blame for what they did. I can and have forgiven those people who have apologized and made amends. I also forgive those who unintentionally hurt me. But, I do not and will not forgive my father or the willing cult members. They now choose to deny or pretend it never happened.

The two main hurts in my life today are physical results of the trauma. I have many health problems and I have been unable to conceive. Since I started remembering the abuse I have been diagnosed with three autoimmune diseases, one of which I still have. I am frequently sick, and I take much longer to get better than most people. I had surgery to fix a 21-year-old damaged jaw from repeated oral rape. I have had five abdominal surgeries. I lost a portion of my intestine due to scarring. I have been infertile due to scarring and have been going through in vitro fertilization due to complications caused by the abuse. I have just recently learned that I am three weeks pregnant, finally, but they are very worried about the possibility of a problem with the pregnancy and with how ill and depleted my body has become.

I feel very angry at my father because I can do very little to change my body's condition. I have filed a civil suit against my father for medical bills. I have also learned to educate myself about my medical conditions and options. And, I have learned to talk about my fears and pains rather than to suppress them as I had to as a child.

My husband and I have learned through the healing process not to let angers and fears fester. When we have a problem or disagreement we work it out. We have gone through a range from celibacy to normalcy in our sex life, while I healed from the memories. If we can't work it out on our own, we see a mediator. I see no reason why our commitment to each other and our family's mental health would not continue even though we are financially strapped as a result of the expenses of my medical problems and the civil suit against my father.

My younger sister recently told me that she resented all of the attention that my brother and I have gotten because of the incest as children. Though she and I write and talk frequently, she moved to the opposite coast shortly after I started memory work. She never brings it up unless I do. My brother and I were very close allies as children. We tried to help each other as best we could. This has continued off and on through adulthood, although he now has come to a point where he doesn't want to hear anything about our abuse.

I wonder why this is? Why have I surpassed the trauma while my brother and sister haven't. This is a question a lot of us surpassers ask. I don't know the answer for certain, but I speculate that it is a combination of inborn personality, relationships I had in childhood, my faith in God, which my siblings don't have, and a willingness, as an adult, to work hard in spite of the pain of remembering. I, therefore, have been able to heal.

Only mother worked with me to heal. It wasn't easy for either of us, but we've become much closer as a result of the successful effort. Mother's side of the family has remained supportive and loving. Since I filed the civil suit against my father, his side of the family has disowned me. Everyone who believes me supports me, which includes my mother, brother, sister, two cousins, and my godfather, their brother. My godfather is the only one of my father's siblings who stuck by me although he never brings it up unless I do.

I have always had a helping career or job. Today I am a volunteer with the state and county chapters of the National Committee for the Prevention of Child Abuse. I speak to adults and children and I help develop prevention programs, such as a play for elementary school children about child sexual abuse. The worst misconception I hear is that a child who discloses and then is disbelieved by the system or families is worse off, so we shouldn't even talk to child victims or offer them any hope. I feel this is very untrue. Any support, such as listening to the fear, pain, anger, and confusion with sympathy or empathy and offering a view of a different kind of life all provide a ray of hope for the young victim. Children need some hope to hold onto. They are much more resilient than adults believe. When people hear my history they say, "But you're so normal, you'd never know!" I believe I'm like that because although I never told anyone the details, loving people knew I was unhappy and gave me extra loving care and chances to escape. That's another thing; tickets to escape from time to time are hope givers and life savers to child victims.

To help others who have had emotionally stressful childhoods, we should listen without judging. We should not minimize what we hear but accept it, no matter how much it hurts to hear it. Remember, the adult survivor has to live with that pain. We should also be very accepting of the person because she or he probably feels like a freak. Also, offer to give hugs if they want them but, most importantly ask what the survivor needs from us.

I was with my third psychotherapist when I retrieved all of my memories of the satanic abuse, and I remember saying to Jerome, my psychologist, "I used to be proud to be a survivor, but now that's not enough anymore. I don't wish to be defined by what happened to me. I am not Janice, survivor of sexual, satanic, physical and emotional abuse. I am Janice, a wife, trainer, gourmet cook, gardener, and friend, and by the way I survived sexual, satanic, physical and emotional abuse." It was at this point that I knew that I had surpassed everything. After five years of concentrated work, I don't feel that I need therapy anymore.

It was after I knew I had survived everything that I sought a better word to define my history and coined the word surpasser. Now, in my training, I talk about the three stages of those who have been abused: (1) victim, (2) survivor, and (3) surpasser. I have formed my own company with another surpasser. Our company has seminars which educate healthcare providers, massage therapists, and survivors about the effects on the body and mind of survivors of abuse. .

In a sick way, my father's increasing sadism and mental games aimed at confusing me, taught me to hold onto what control I could grasp. It became a test of wills, his to see if he could break me, mine to make sure he didn't see me break. I think this helped me survive. I am very good at problem solving and reaching people. I believe both skills are a result of constantly being on guard and having to assess people and situations for danger. I always had to make a decision between the best of two awful choices.

Also, my mother's traditional training of "Obey your husband or father and don't question" helped me by being a role model for how I should acquiesce and do as I was told in the cult activities. My nature was to fight it, but after trying that once I realized I was safer if I acted like my mother did at home. I believe it saved my life many times.

Hopefully, I'll be able to carry this pregnancy to term. Since I have been in therapy, I know that I will never repeat the cycle of abuse. I may not always be able to control my temper when my kids are screaming and the rest of my life is boiling over, but I have the tools to not repeat my father's behavior.

I am living proof that you can survive and surpass trauma. My life has been very hard and will always continue to be so because of the trauma my body has endured. The negative effects are physical and financial, and of course this has placed a great deal of stress on my marriage. But, I am very happy with my life in spite of everything, and I am coping well despite all the stresses and know that my husband and I will survive and surpass any coming hardships. Our marriage is stronger, we believe, because of the process of healing. And, as I always say when everything seems to be going wrong, "This too shall pass. Some other shit will come along to take its place, but I'll get through it and beyond it."

All in all, I believe it has made me a better person, committed to educating and helping others. I can care about others without caring at the expense of myself. My life now has a healthy balance. I am no longer obsessive or controlling. When normal life crises occur I can cope well without retreating to childlike behavior, regressing, or dissociating.

In the future I will continue running my company and doing my volunteer prevention work to educate adults about the effects of abuse on adult lives. I will always look for and encourage the good in people, because I believe they are born inherently that way, and if loved and cherished will not become evil. I am a living testimony to that. I not only figured out how to survive the abuse, but I did so without becoming evil myself, and I am very proud of that. In having seen the dark side of people I am even more determined to seek the light.

If I want good things, good people, or anything good in my life, I must be good myself and be able to share my goodness in my world. Most importantly, I have surpassed my childhood trauma! If I can do that I can get through the rest of life's problems. I am lovable and good!

I AM A WALKING MIRACLE; IT HELPS ME BELIEVE IN OTHER MIRACLES

Deserted by her mother, placed in an orphanage by her father, unloved by her three brothers and sister, and disliked by the nuns and other institutionalized children, this fifty-year-old bicultural professional woman tells how she survived and transcended her lonely childhood:

Our mother left the four of us when my two brothers were ages six and three and my twin sister and I were age four. We weren't left alone, however, for our father got custody. But, with no help, he was forced to put us into institutions, the boys in a boys' home and my twin and me in a girls' home. We were there nine years.

Actually, he didn't abandon us entirely. He came and saw us once a week.

Sometimes we'd even go home with him for the weekend where, as time went by, I was the "mother" figure as I did most of the cleaning, etc. Until then our dad gave us basic care, he cooked for us and provided a place for us to be all together. He slept on chairs while the four of us slept in his bed. He was very gentle.

What was rough on me was that I never fit in those nine years. No one liked me, not the nuns or the other kids, and what's hardest of all, not my twin sister. I was extremely lonely. I cried almost every night. I was not included in little groups at the home and when we went home with dad on weekends; my brothers and sister were closer to each other than they were to me. My sister and my youngest brother were like twins, they did everything together.

I was judged as being weird by my family and acquaintances. I was always told that I talked too much. Others were always categorizing me and criticizing me for not meeting their expectations. When others acted superior to me I felt I was being treated like dirt, like a dog. Oh, how I hate to be looked down upon and called "poor kid." Shit! No one ever saw the good I did. And no one ever listened to me. My only saving grace was being a good student and escaping into books, songs, and prayer and seeing dad once a week.

Though living at the home, we went to a regular Catholic grade school a block away. I soon found that I could get some satisfaction in my lonely life by being a good student. And, out of all my teachers, two nuns in the fifth and seventh grade liked me. Even the one nun who was very rough on us liked and respected me as a student in the eighth grade. At one point I was the top student at the school. But, what furthered my feelings of alienation at the home was my being a "brown" kid. Our father was Filipino, though our mother was a Norwegian-German mix. There were only six of us "brown" kids in the home and we were discriminated against at times. Also, we lived in a black area. We couldn't live in a white area as we were Filipino filth. Yet, I kept going to school and working hard and eventually I learned how to do good for others, even though others weren't doing good for me. I tried to do positive things and not pay back bad for bad. In the home we were taught to be "guardian angels" to the new girls when they came in, and to look out for them. Most of them only stayed in the home one to three years but we were there nine years. The rest of the time I would go for walks alone, pray, and sing, and I would read, read, read.

When we went to public high school we left the home and lived, once again, with our father. Those four years were lost, lonely years. After nine years in an institution, my twin and I didn't know how to get along. We never did anything together though we slept in the same bed. I wish we could have had fun times together and shared, like other sisters do. We never tried on make-up together or went shopping or anything. I so wished that we had a mother or an older woman to confide in. Of course, I had turned to Our Lady (Blessed Mother) as a child when I had no human mother to turn to, but a real person could have helped us with female concerns. She could have helped us know how to dress, etc. In the home the nuns taught us to wear the same outfits over and over again, one outfit for three days and another one for the other two days of school each week. So in high school when we had four to six different outfits to wear, we still wore them the same way we had learned our whole four years in the home. Again, I did well in school. I maintained a B average and kept up my prayers and reading.

I didn't date until after high school. Then I took up with a high school dropout and stuck with him for three years. There was no real communication in that relationship. I had rough relationships from ages 17 to 25. I was used and mistreated emotionally and physically, but I was looking for love, for someone to love me for who I was and to love me unconditionally. I was so desperately wanted someone to hold me and it was a way to be held, but with hardly any sexual fulfillment. However, I was used and made to feel cheap by giving in and doing for men, although it takes two to tango. I did get five marriage proposals though during this time, and I was the one who broke up with them, not they with me. I can take not being held if the reason isn't rejection of me but for another person. I was rejected like that by my husband. Yikes!

Those post–high school years were probably my most traumatic times, as that was when I walked away from the practice of my religion. I didn't go to church for 8 years and I had no sacraments for 16 years. Still, I was very disciplined. I'd go to work, go to school, and take care of the house, etc., and fall apart in between. I felt I was in trouble though, and definitely not approved of. I used to yell, scream and cry, and bang my head against the wall to try and get some relief from my emotional pain. These were the times when I hurt myself the most and when I let others hurt me the most. It was also the time that I made a serious attempt at suicide. Ironically, this was also the time that I had my first real friend, someone who truly listened to me. I was almost in a state of shock. It was like going from dark into light, two-way communication. I guess this friendship came a little late for me though. I still felt I was giving so many people trouble, my boyfriend, my family, and even my first real friend, that I thought I'd save the world some trouble and kill myself. I was 20 years old and at my friend's house, and I remember running from the bedroom to the kitchen and taking a kitchen knife and chopping away at my wrist and arm. For some reason it made me think of my dad hacking away at a chicken. Anyway, the knife turned out to be too dull to do any harm and I have very deep veins, so I didn't succeed in hurting myself in the way I'd intended. My family was very upset that I dared to make a serious attempt at suicide. I saw a psychiatrist for two months after that. He was a good listener.

As I mentioned before, I got married. All I wanted since I was put in the home was to get married and have 12 kids. This was one reason that my twin didn't like me or have much to do with me when we were growing up. She thought this was a weird dream. But, I wanted the home and the family I didn't have when I was growing up. That marriage didn't work out but I did get three children out of the relationship. Even that part of my life wasn't easy. I miscarried four times, only two are on record. After three years of marriage and no children, I decided to adopt. I knew that sooner or later I'd hold on to a biological kid. So, between my third and fourth year of marriage I adopted two little girls. It was hard being a mother to kids, especially daughters, as I never had that relationship. I really had serious problems raising them, but I wouldn't walk away as I saw what happened to my mother. I just seem to have more distance with girls, yet, one of my closest friends is a girl. It was because of them, however, that I went back to my religion. There was no way I was going to try and raise them without a religion, so back to weekly mass, and so on, I went. Faith, discipline, and doing for others made the difference, so I was able to raise my daughters and survive myself. It was when I discovered Jesus' unconditional love that I was on the way to deeper healing.

Soon, I did give birth to a baby boy. They are now 19, 21, and 23 years of age, and I have one grandchild.

After finally sharing my story with a friend, who accepted me and my kids as we were and still thought us neat people, I could then write my story about my nine years in an orphanage in book form, letter style, 26 pages in all. My girls have read my story. Also, I've always been open about my past. My son, however, isn't quite ready to read my story. Yet, he knows it.

I know now that my dad cared for me, and even my brothers and my twin sister cared for me in their own special ways when I was growing up. My intelligence and especially my gift of being able to be forgiving of others has helped me to finally get closer to my family. I know that others hurt you because they themselves are hurting. So I'm so glad that I was able to take care of my dad when he was dying. At the time it was really rough for me, because I was also taking care of my three kids and going to college. But, all the years he struggled to raise us the best he could and he never really turned us against our mother. I only saw her twice in 17 years, when I was 9 and 13, but we wrote to each other. Also, we occasionally saw her family. They weren't ashamed of us because we were part Filipino. They were proud of us. That is why I was able to forgive my mother for abandoning us. I moved to California to get to know my mother. She overreacted to my hurts, etc., out of guilt. Yet, I kept going back. At one point she said that I was her favorite, that's because I could accept the good and the "hurting" part of her. When she died, I put her ashes up on a mountain top. She was the best grandparent to my adopted daughters. I try to help others know they can love and accept parents who left them. I did.

My childhood experiences have given me a special way of relating to others from all backgrounds. It has given me faith to build on. It has given me discipline and the ability to compartmentalize my life. (We were regulated from morning to night in the home.) It has given me special childhood connections with my twin and my brothers and even my cousins. It has given me compassion for other hurting individuals. I do not forget the hurts, the doing without, but I look at things in a more positive way as I reach out naturally to others in hurting situations. I have done more, seen more, and am living my life to the fullest with God's loving help. Without being able to forgive, one can't experience real happiness and peace.

Most of my real lasting healing has taken place in the last 5 years. Yes, there are some negative effects still present from my childhood; they are always a part of me. But most I've worked out except for my fear of closed spaces. I vaguely remember being locked in a bathroom and screaming. Yikes! I mix well with others but I also need my time alone. I've been alone most of my life, 9 years in an institution, 4 years of high school, 12 years of marriage to a man who worked nights, and being divorced the rest of the time. I am now in a committed relationship, and even though I am celibate I feel more fulfilled, more attractive, and sexier then ever. Sex is mainly feeling good about being female or male and what goes with it. Being loved, as is, without demands, without being expected to be perfect. What a gift.

My relationships with my family members have gotten better over the years. For myself, I've kept a daily journal for the last 12 years. But to others I am open and quite the letter writer. I just sent out 21 friendly pieces of mail last week. I am also a phone caller, so we are forever getting closer. I just went back to Vermont and New York to visit relatives at Christmas and New Year's and saw cousins I hadn't seen in 12 years. Some I hadn't seen in 27 years. They all treated me well, including my brothers and their families. They are much more gentle with me now. I'm even like the go-between for some relatives, cousin to cousin, aunt, brothers. I help them to get closer to each other. It's really neat to be loved by all.

I've had many jobs over the years from a waitress to a keypuncher to an English teacher. But I kept going to school and found I had a real love for teaching special education classes. I remember my psychiatrist, at one point being afraid I would go schizophrenic on him and be in a corner by myself. Even the director of my school district couldn't believe it when I was hired to teach special education and now sees where I am today. I have a BA in English, an MA in education, my teaching credentials in English, Spanish, and learning handicapped, plus a resource specialist certificate. And, of course, I have my three children, one grandchild, and friends galore, and a family that loves me. I own my own home, two cars, and a spa I just had put in last year.

Mainly, my childhood has had positive effects on me. I got faith, compassion, and an ability to accept others. My institutional background gave me more tolerance for crazy behaviors. I don't see myself burning out of special education like others, as I'm disciplined, organized, and have an ability to forgive others and especially myself. I hurt when I see my kids accept being mistreated. I hurt when others are hurt and mistreated due to color, learning disability, etc. I hurt when schools discriminate against kids from racially mixed or deprived backgrounds. I expect everyone to achieve to the best of their abilities. I believe all can be educated and I accept differences in people. I will never call anyone poor kid, nor will I look down on anyone as was done to me. Kids can survive and achieve if someone believes in them and gives them a chance.

These are things I now believe: life will have pain, but life can be so beautiful; people can be so kind, so thoughtful, so caring; little things do mean a lot; and being accepted as you are helps you to grow to your fullest potential. I also wholeheartedly believe that I am great and that I have always been liked by some people and that people like me as I like myself. I make a point to try and not judge others, although I'm sure I do at times. I am now aware that when people hurt others it is because they are hurting inside themselves. I know that I am strong. I am a survivor. I am a walking miracle. It helps me believe in other miracles.

Chapter 9

What We Have Learned

Now it is time to step back and think broadly about what we have learned and how these findings can be used in our society to better serve children and adults who experienced a traumatic childhood. The ninety adults, who told us, in-depth, about their traumatic childhood, focused on many issues that can be summarized as we review answers to a number of succinct questions that we posed at the beginning of the research:

What happened?
When did this happen? When did it end?
What are the common feelings associated with trauma?
Who helped?
What helped during childhood?
Who are they today?
What helped during adulthood?
What can we do to help children survive and adults transcend?
Let us go back and briefly report what we learned from the participants as they answered each of our questions:

WHAT HAPPENED

The trauma experienced by the participants in this study, in every case but one, included some form of abuse. The trauma and abuse was most often inflicted by family members. We were surprised to learn that most of the participants experienced many forms of abuse in their childhood with half of the participants experiencing six to ten

Surviving and Transcending a Traumatic Childhood
© 2007 by The Haworth Press, Inc. All rights reserved.
doi:10.1300/5839_09

forms of abuse. For example, if there was alcohol or drug abuse there also might be violence, neglect, and emotional abuse. This meant that for many of the participants, they were experiencing abuse in many aspects of their lives. They could not avoid it. Emotional abuse was the most frequently cited form of trauma (87.7 percent of the participants experienced this), followed by physical abuse (64.4 percent), violence (63.3 percent), sexual abuse (52.2 percent), alcohol or other drug abuse in the family (51.1 percent), abandonment (48.8 percent), alienation (47.7 percent), and neglect (47.7 percent).

These findings struck us as especially poignant and can be stated in this way: Abuse was the most common form of trauma children experienced, and the abuse was most likely to be inflicted by those who are supposed to love them and care for them.

WHEN IT HAPPENED
AND WHEN IT ENDED

We were very interested in learning how long a traumatic childhood lasts. For most of the participants, trauma was always there as a youngster, and had been going on as long as they could remember. They were born into a life of difficulties and we wondered where they found the hope that things would ever get better.

On average, individuals believed the traumatic times began at 4.9 years of age and ended when they were 24.0 years. That is an average of 19 years of trauma to endure. All the participants made it very clear to us that the aftermath of the childhood trauma lasts forever. It truly is the dark thread that will always be part of one's life, and that is not all bad. The trauma in their childhood is part of who they are today.

COMMON FEELINGS
ASSOCIATED WITH TRAUMA

The pain associated with the individuals' memories of childhood was sometimes staggering for them to recall, and can be grouped into six categories: (1) loneliness and isolation; (2) fear and confusion; (3) bitterness, anger, and sorrow; (4) skepticism and distrust; (5) feeling like I might go crazy; and (6) guilt and blame. The feelings are not likely to go away, but they do lose their intensity and control over the individual's life, as time goes by and the person learns valuable lessons about life.

PEOPLE WHO HELPED

Emotional pain can be as devastating as physical pain, and we come away from this study concluding that though many individuals suffered considerable physical trauma to their bodies, the damage to their spirit was more devastating. Reading the stories of the participants, one is continually struck by how *alone* most of them felt. The majority of the participants in this study (56 percent) had no one who would or could listen to them during their troubled time as children. Others reported that they had someone who would listen: 20 percent said there was someone in the family to turn to; 9 percent cited teachers; 5 percent said friends; 3 percent checked "other"; 2 percent said professional counselors; no one cited clergy.

Feelings of alienation and fear of being alone or being isolated from those who could give support were very common. Participants talked about relief or the "vacation" that was provided when someone befriended them. It did not mean the person made the abuse stop, but as children were able to feel accepted and could have glimpses of what life could be like. This sense of connection, support, and comfort in the world helped them endure the situation.

FACTORS THAT HELPED
DURING CHILDHOOD

Key elements in the process of surviving and transcending can be broken down into five areas: (1) spiritual resources, (2) dissociation, (3) escape, (4) accepting life as it is, and (5) survival by default.

Religion or *spirituality* was mentioned by nearly everyone in the study, though beliefs and approaches varied considerably. Clergy were not a source of support during childhood, but a spiritual sense was helpful: "God" or "a higher being" gave a great amount of comfort and hope to these lost souls forced to suffer in silence. If you have no control over your world, you are forced to create a version of a higher power that would be in control, a power that had the traits of love, kindness, and other positive qualities that were likely to be absent in your family.

The participants in this study reported that without the power to create a safe and loving world for themselves, they were many times forced to *dissociate* from the experience, to emotionally disappear. Many of the participants told of how they would *escape* the nightmare of their life by disappearing into books or the beauty of nature. Another strategy was to focus on schoolwork and school activities, or work especially hard to become really good at something and receive praise for their efforts outside their home.

With no power or control over the situation, many were simply forced to *accept life as it was,* because there was no way out and no other reality possible for them. Were the events viewed as traumatic when they were experiencing them? Forty-seven percent of the respondents said "no." They explained that they had limited experience in life and no other perspective from which to judge their situation. Genuine help for the children in these situations was simply not there. The world apparently was looking the other way.

Finally, as children they *survived by default.* There was nothing planned or thought out. Sometimes it was pure luck that kept them from being hurt or even killed. To use the word *cope* here would not be precise, because that implies rationality and control over the situation to some degree. Adults cope. Children *endure.* They made choices as the options were placed in front of them. Do I go hide in the closet to avoid a beating, or do I stay and take it? Who knows what would be the best choice? So they respond with what was close at hand and lived with the consequences, knowing that the consequences were likely to be negative either way.

WHO THEY ARE TODAY

When did they move from simply surviving to transcending? How did it happen? Each story is different but, generally speaking, this happened when they became free enough to distance themselves emotionally and physically from the source of their trauma. Even though most believed they had risen above the trauma of the past, nearly everyone had answers for our question, "What still hurts today?" Even though they generally felt they were doing well in life as adults, they still felt the impact of their childhood trauma would never completely go away.

Seventy-three percent of the participants said that the traumatic experiences as children had made them better people. When asked how the trauma affected their lives in the final analysis, 64 percent said the effects were a combination of both negative and positive; 23 percent said all positive, and 13 percent said all negative. When asked, "How do you know you're really okay today?" most indicated by saying that they were alive, they were able to function in the world, and they were continuing on in the process of transcending.

We were interested in the strengths of their family of origin today, and we wanted to see if the participants sensed positive changes. The majority of people said their family of origin had "no strengths" today. Scattered responses focused on "a family member who is supportive," "a strong work ethic" in the family of origin today, and "my mother's organizational ability." Also listed as strengths were "structure" and "rigidity," but for the most part, families of origin were not seen as particularly healthy. Participants also talked about some of their siblings who had not transcended, but continued the cycle of abuse.

Nearly three-fourths of the participants had children (74.7 percent). Many of the accounts of the survivors who became parents were positive, but the carryover of the trauma was still present. Were they worried about falling into a vicious cycle of abuse and passing on the pain they experienced in their families of origin to their own children? Forty percent said they did worry about intergenerational transmission of past problems, while 56 percent said they were not worried. A few chose not to have children at all.

The statistics from the participants give a powerful picture of the survivors. Even with the fears and phobias, the flashbacks, and dreams, there is an ongoing sense of transcending by the majority of the respondents. They commonly believed they would continue to deal with the issues surrounding the trauma for the rest of their lives. The picture is very, very complex.

FACTORS THAT HELPED
DURING ADULTHOOD

The participants discussed the things that they felt helped them transcend a traumatic childhood during their adult years. The five things talked about most often were: (1) spirituality, (2) therapy and/or support groups, (3) getting married, (4) escaping from the abuse, and (5) looking forward not back.

Every respondent was affected by religion and/or *spirituality* as they moved through the process of transcending. Religion was rarely a positive factor in transcending the trauma, but spirituality was helpful. Spirituality was at first a source of comfort and a way to get through the difficult times. As they progressed through the healing process they talked about spirituality helping them to understand what had happened to them and to think about their suffering in new ways.

Fifty-seven percent of the participants in the study had contemplated suicide because of what had happened to them as children. Nineteen percent had actually tried to kill themselves. These are understandable mental health symptoms of the trauma and indicate the importance of professional help. We learned that 64 percent of the participants in this study sought the guidance of a *therapist* who was helpful in the process of transcending. They usually went to a therapist out of desperation, unable to control the pain, sadness, lack of sleep, nightmares, or depression. The rest of the participants (36 percent) did not seek the help of a therapist in transcending their traumatic childhoods. Some said they would not have made it without the help of a therapist; others expressed pride at having made the journey on their own. Also, 51 percent of the participants attended a *support group* in the process of transcending, attending an average of twenty-six meetings. Some saw a therapist *and* attended support group meetings. Others only saw a therapist or attended support group meetings, but not both. The healing process, even with the help of a therapist, was very slow.

Seventy percent of those who participated in our study said their childhood experiences affected their decision to be involved in a committed relationship or to marry. For some, it meant that they were afraid to trust another person; for others, it meant they wanted a happy *marriage* and family life because they had not experienced a healthy family life as a child. Out of the ninety participants, eighty

(93 percent) had been married at least once. Of those who had been married at least once, 49 percent felt that marriage was helpful in transcending their traumatic childhoods. Sometimes they found this help in their first marriage and some found it in a subsequent marriage. Sometimes their first marriage was just as bad as the family where they grew up, but it may have been the first step in moving away from the family where the abuse occurred. On average, participants in this study were married 1.3 times.

Moving away or *escaping from the abuse* came when they were 18 years old as they went off to college, work, or the military. Even though we did not specifically ask the participants if moving away was a strategy they used to transcend a traumatic childhood, 44 percent of the participants in the study volunteered that moving away and/or severing contact was a critical part of transcending. They often times went into the world with fears about what life had to hold and were ill-prepared emotionally, socially, and financially. They saw the move, however, as a more positive alternative than continuing to stay where the abuse could continue.

Some of the people in the study (24 percent) said that looking forward to positive things, rather than dwelling on the past, was one of the things that helped them transcend a traumatic childhood. These participants were likely to have examined what had happened to them, begun to heal, and wanted to move to a place where there was less emotional pain. Generally speaking, they had a positive attitude toward life and viewed the future with a sense of hope. The advice they gave was to move on, let go of the past, and not to use it as an excuse for failure.

See Exhibit 9.1, What Have We Learned?, for a concise summary of the findings of this research. The findings are divided into two sections: Surviving the Trauma as Children, and Transcending the Trauma as Adults. Also, see Exhibit 9.2, Wise Counsel, for a collection of great advice from the participants in this study.

HELPING CHILDREN SURVIVE
AND ADULTS TRANSCEND

Perhaps the most distressing thing we learned from the participants in this study of surviving and transcending a traumatic childhood was

EXHIBIT 9.1. What Have We Learned? A Very Brief Summary

SURVIVING THE TRAUMA AS CHILDREN

- Abuse is the most common form of trauma children suffer, and the abuse is very likely to be inflicted by those who are supposed to love you and care for them.
- A traumatic childhood often begins when they are so young they cannot even remember the beginning, and it ends an average of almost twenty years later when you escape from the abusive situation as a young adult. The aftermath of the childhood trauma, however, lasts forever.
- Extraordinarily strong feelings are associated with the individual's memories of traumatic childhood, including: (1) loneliness and isolation; (2) fear and confusion; (3) bitterness, anger, and sorrow; (4) skepticism and distrust; (5) feeling like I might go crazy; and (6) guilt and blame. The person is not likely to forget these memories, but it is possible to find ways to manage these emotions in effective and life-affirming ways.
- Reading the stories of the participants, one is continually struck by how *alone* most of them felt as children. The majority (56 percent) reported there was no one who would or could listen to them during this time. Others had someone to talk to: 20 percent said there was someone in the family to turn to; 9 percent cited teachers; 5 percent said friends; 3 percent checked "other"; 2 percent said professional counselors; no one cited clergy.
- What helped? Key elements in the process of surviving as children can be broken down into five areas: (1) spiritual resources, (2) dissociation, (3) escape, (4) accepting life as it is, and (5) survival by default.
- Children in the same family can react in very different ways to the trauma. Some identify with the perpetrator and grow into perpetrators themselves. Others make a conscious decision to identify with the good in life and become public servants of one kind or another.
- We can help children survive by befriending them and showing care and concern, and giving them a glimpse of what life can be like.

TRANSCENDING THE TRAUMA AS ADULTS

- It takes a long time to heal.
- There are many paths along the journey of healing. What works for one is not necessarily what works for another.
- "Why did this happen to me?" In the final analysis answering "the why question" may never be truly possible. The more useful question to ask may be, "Where do I go from here?"

- At the end of the research process, we asked the individuals one more time if they continued to believe that they had both survived *and* transcended their traumatic childhood. Fully 83 percent concluded that they had, indeed, survived *and* transcended. Six percent did not answer the question, and 11 percent said they had only survived.
- When did they move from simply surviving to transcending? How did it happen? Each story is different but, generally speaking, this happened when they became free enough to distance themselves emotionally and physically from the source of their trauma.
- Even though most believed they had risen above the trauma of the past, nearly everyone could give examples of things that still hurt today. They generally felt they were doing well in life as adults, but they still felt the impact of their childhood trauma.
- Seventy-two percent said they still experienced personal guilt associated with what had happened in their lives.
- Seventy-three percent of the participants said that the traumatic experiences as children had made them better people.
- When asked how the trauma affected their lives in the final analysis, 64 percent said the effects were a combination of both negative and positive; 23 percent said all positive, and 13 percent said all negative.
- When asked, "How do you know you're really okay today?" most indicated by saying that they were alive, they were able to function in the world, and they were continuing on in the process of transcending.
- We were interested in the strengths of their family of origin today, for we wanted to see if the participants sensed positive changes. The majority of people said their family of origin had "no strengths" today.
- Most of the participants (56 percent) were not worried that they would fall into a vicious cycle of abuse and pass on the pain and disorder of their childhood to their own children. However, 40 percent said they did worry about intergenerational transmission of past problems.
- People sometimes hurt themselves to escape emotional pain. They also sometimes let others hurt them in a way to escape guilt and pain: "I was used and mistreated emotionally and physically, but I was looking for love, for someone to love me for who I was and to love me unconditionally."
- Drinking and other drug abuses were other unsuccessful ways they try to escape from emotional pain.
- Transcending was a very long, difficult, and painful process. Although one may become what is considered a healthy adult, the trauma and the effects of the trauma never completely go away. The trauma or abuse will always be the dark thread in the tapestry.

(continued)

(continued)

- Who was responsible for the growth, the change? These individuals told us, basically, that they had to do it for themselves. They got help
- from many good people, but in the final analysis as one woman said, "The key person is me." Individuals transcended because *they* made it happen.
- The participants identified things that they felt helped them transcend a traumatic childhood during their adult years. The five most common aids to transcending were: (1) spirituality, (2) therapy and/or support groups, (3) getting married, (4) escaping from the abuse, and (5) looking forward not back.
- Fifty-seven percent had thought about committing suicide because of what had happened to them. Nineteen percent had actually tried to kill themselves at some point. These are understandable mental health symptoms of the trauma experienced by those who participated in the study.
- We can help adults transcend by listening as they tell their story and responding positively. This will help them in the process of transcending.

EXHIBIT 9.2. Wise Counsel

The participants in this study often said wonderful, wise things that need to be repeated. Here is a collection of our favorites with some of our own commentary added:

- *Let go and let God.* There are just some things that we are not in control of, and that is alright.
- *Forgive, but we cannot forget.* We can let go of our anger and hatred, but memories will always remain and that is okay.
- *Forgiveness is the first step in learning to love oneself and in learning to love others.* Thus, transcending implies forgiveness. We need to forgive ourselves and we need to forgive the abuser.
- *Wherever we go, there we are.* We cannot run away from ourselves and our problems.
- We are only unique in the details, not the general experience of life. Human beings are much more similar than different, and that is why we can, for the most part, understand each other.
- *And the truth shall set us free.* It is important to understand what has happened.

- *Accentuate the positive.* Explore negative experiences, but grow past them. Focus on where we are going in life, and do not get totally bogged down in where we have been.
- *Life is a process. Changes can happen if we learn how to make changes ourselves.*
- *The dark thread can never be removed, and it should not be removed.* What happened has made us who we are today.
- *Life is, in large part, what we make of it.* There are many things we cannot control, but there are a surprising number of things in life that we can influence to a significant extent.
- *Others hurt us because they themselves are hurting.* Those who hurt us had probably been hurt. To escape our own emotional pain, we sometimes try to hurt other people.
- [An especially good summary of advice from one individual] *Accept, forgive, and forget as much as possible. Don't give up, look forward not back, but do not forget the good or the bad. Make do with what you have and always believe in yourself. Be a good person and never give up, read a lot, stay with reality, be yourself. Be on top and do not let other people put you down.*
- *Faith, discipline, and doing for others made the difference.* Many people help themselves to heal by dedicating themselves to helping others, working as counselors, as teachers, working with children, being good friends to others, and so forth.
- *Each child is like a snowflake, no two are alike.* Adults need to know this if they are to work successfully with children, especially those who have been traumatized.

how many people were aware of the trauma the children were suffering, and how few people actually tried to help. The trauma described in these pages happened many years ago, twenty, thirty, forty, fifty years and more, so one might argue that today is different, today is better for children. Probably not, we would guess.

During catastrophic times today, we see enormous outpourings of goodness in American culture. Bravery and generosity of spirit are regularly in evidence: a child is drowning in a lake and an adult is quick to try to save her; a family is stricken by flood, fire, and countless other types of tragedy, and many good souls are quick to offer assistance. And yet, we wonder if the basic attitude toward the family—that it is a private place where outsiders are not supposed to tread—may be very similar to what it was in the past. Today, it still seems too easy to look the other way, too easy to reassure ourselves that violence and abuse are not happening in a family we know, and change the channel in our minds to another more reassuring and positive thought. We just wonder about this.

If the world really is to become a better place for children, especially children in great distress, it will take a dedicated family of humankind to be constantly vigilant on behalf of all children. It will take considerable effort for each of us to find the courage to intervene on behalf of each child we suspect is at risk.

We can also befriend or be kind to children who we sense need special care. We can give them time, attention, and unconditional love. Many of the participants in this study remembered the kindness shown to them by a friend, relative, teacher, or neighbor. It gave them an opportunity to experience something in life that made them feel loved and cared for; it let them know that there were other ways to live.

The participants in this study also gave us guidance about how we can respond to adults as they transcend. They told us to listen as they tell their story and to react positively. One woman told us that when she told a friend about her childhood, the friend still "accepted me and thought us neat people." Others told us to "validate their worth," because they may not have experienced that before. We may be the first person in their life who has helped them begin to feel whole.

We hope personally, however, that we will never forget the stories in this book and the images they forced upon us. The terror is real, the tragedy is endless. Will each of us have the courage and goodness of spirit to respond?

Appendix A

Selected Readings

ALCOHOL AND THE ABUSE OF OTHER DRUGS

Al-Anon/Alateen. Welcome to Al-Anon and Alateen. www.al-anon.alateen
.org
   For spouses and children of alcoholics and problem drinkers.

Alcohol Free Children. How does alcohol affect the world of a child.
http://www.alcoholfreechildren.org/gs/pubs/html/Stat.htm
   This organization compiles excellent information on children and
   family issues related to alcohol.

Alcoholics Anonymous. http:///www.alcoholics-anonymous.org/
   Information from the pioneering organization.

Allsop, S., & Saunders, B. (1989). Relapse and alcohol problems. In M.
   Gossop (Ed.), *Relapse and addictive behaviour* (pp. 11-40). New York:
   Tavistock/Routledge.

Ennett, S. T., Bauman, K. E., Foshee, V. A., Pemberton, M., & Hicks, K. A.
   (2001). Parent-child communication about adolescent tobacco and alcohol use: What do parents say and does it affect youth behavior? *Journal
   of Marriage and Family, 63*(February), 48-62.
   Parents have to be careful about how they advise their teenagers, because the young people sometimes do the exact opposite of what parents suggest.

National Council on Alcoholism and Drug Dependence (NCADD). Alcohol and drug dependence are America's number one health problem.
   http://www.ncaad.org/facts/numbroneproblem.html

Surviving and Transcending a Traumatic Childhood
© 2007 by The Haworth Press, Inc. All rights reserved.
doi:10.1300/5839_10

National Institute on Alcohol Abuse and Alcoholism. Alcohol problems in intimate relationships: Identification and intervention. http://www.niaaa .nih.gov/publications/niaaa-guide/
   A guide for marriage and family therapists.

O'Farrell, T. J., & Fals-Stewart, W. (2001). Family-involved alcoholism treatment: An update. *Recent Developments in Alcoholism, 15,* 329-356.

CHILD MALTREATMENT

Administration for Children and Families. Child maltreatment 2002. U.S. Department of Health and Human Services. Washington, DC. www .afterschool.gov/xhtmL/Topic/t_9.html

Administration for Children and Families. Protecting the WellBeing of Children. U.S. Department of Health and Human Services. Washington, D.C. www.Acf.hhs.gov/news/facts/chilwelf.html

American Academy of Child and Adolescent Psychiatry. Child sexual abuse. from http://www.aacap.org/publications/factsfam/sexabuse.html

Straus, M. A., & Field, C. J. (2003). Psychological aggression by American parents: National data on prevalence, chronicity, and severity. *Journal of Marriage and Family, 65*(November), 795-808.

United Way of Central New Mexico. Sibling abuse. http://www.uwcnm .org/information/siblingabuse.html

DEATH, DYING, AND BEREAVEMENT

Aiken, L. R. (2004). *Dying, death, and bereavement* (4th ed.). Mahwah, NJ: Lawrence Erlbaum Associates.
   A brief but comprehensive survey of research, writings, and professional practices on death and dying.

Compassionate Friends. http://www.compassionatefriends.org/
   A national nonprofit, self-help support organization that offers friendship, understanding, and hope to bereaved parents, grandparents, and others. There is no religious affiliation and there are no membership dues or fees.

Kübler-Ross, E. & Kessler, D. (2000). *Life lessons: Two experts on death and dying teach us about the mysteries of life and living*, New York: Scribner.

M.I.S.S. Foundation. http://www.missfoundation.org/
A nonprofit, 501(c)3, international organization which provides immediate and ongoing support to grieving families, empowerment through community volunteerism opportunities, public policy and legislative education, and programs to reduce infant and toddler death through research and education.

DIVORCE, SINGLE PARENTHOOD, AND STEPFAMILIES

Clapp, G. (2000). *Divorce and new beginnings: A complete guide to recovery. Solo parenting, co-parenting, and stepfamilies* (2nd ed.). New York: Wiley.
Offers guidelines for navigating the difficult straits of loss, growth, and resolution.

Coltrane, S., & Adams, M. (2003). The social construction of the divorce "problem": Morality, child victims, and the politics of gender. *Family Relations, 52*(4), 363-372.
Argues that much of contemporary America's interest in the divorce "problem" and the so-called breakdown of the family is politically motivated and led by conservative organizations bent on portraying children as victims of divorce and masking the underlying issue of gender inequality.

Hetherington, E. M., & Stanley-Hagan, M. M. (2000). Divorce. In A. E. Kazdin (Ed.), *Encyclopedia of Psychology, 3* (pp. 61-65). Washington, DC: American Psychological Association/Oxford University Press.
A useful synopsis.

Jones, A. C. (2003). Reconstructing the stepfamily: Old myths, new stories. *Social Work, 48*(2), 228-237.
A new look at an old family form.

Wallerstein, J. S., & Blakeslee, S. (2003). *What about the kids? Raising your children before, during, and after divorce.* New York: Hyperion.
Wallerstein and her colleagues have devoted many years to learning about the process of divorce and effects on family members.

DOMESTIC VIOLENCE

Bancroft, L. (2002). *Why does he do that? Inside the minds of angry and controlling men*. New York: Putnam's Sons.
Helps us understand the mind and motives of the batterer.

Bushman, B. J., & Anderson, C. A. (2001). Media violence and the American public: Scientific facts versus media misinformation. *American Psychologist, 56*(6/7), 477-489.
Media violence is clearly linked to violence in our society, but the media do not clearly report this fact.

Carp, F. M. (2000). *Elder abuse in the family: An interdisciplinary model for research*. New York: Springer.

Emery, R. E., & Laumann-Billings, L. (1998). An overview of the nature, causes, and consequences of abusive family relationships. *American Psychologist, 53*(2), 121-135.

Goetting, A. (1999). *Getting out: Life stories of women who left abusive men*. New York: Columbia University Press.
The biographies of a small sample of women who escaped from abusive men, usually their husbands.

Graham-Bermann, S. A., & Edleson, J. L. (Eds.) (2001). *Domestic violence in the lives of children: The future of research, intervention, and social policy*. Washington, DC: American Psychological Association Books.
For researchers, policymakers, and those who care about the effects of domestic violence on children.

Malley-Morrison, K. (2003). *Family violence in a cultural perspective: Defining, understanding, and combating abuse*. Thousand Oaks, CA: Sage.
Focuses on family violence from four major ethnic populations in the United States: Native Americans, African Americans, Hispanic-Latinos, and Asian Americans.

Schewe, P. A. (2002). *Preventing violence in relationships: Interventions across the life span*. Washington, DC: American Psychological Association.
Focuses on healthy interpersonal relationship skills as the basis for preventing violence.

Ulman, A., & Straus, M. A. (2003). Violence by children against mothers in relation to violence between parents and corporal punishment by parents. *Journal of Comparative Family Studies, 34*(1), 41-60.

Vincent, J. P., & Jouriles, E. N. (2000). *Domestic violence: Guidelines for research-informed practice.* London and Philadelphia: Jessica Kingsley Publishers.

Walker, L. E. (2000). *The battered woman syndrome* (2nd ed.). New York: Springer.

ETHNIC AND CULTURAL ISSUES

Barnes, S. L. (2001). Stressors and strengths: A theoretical and practical examination of nuclear, single-parent, and augmented African American families. *Families in Society: The Journal of Contemporary Human Services, 82*(5), 449-460.
Academic studies of African American families have focused on the negative for many years. This study takes a more balanced approach, looking at both family problems and successes.

Rosenblatt, P. C., Karis, T., & Powell, R. D. (1995). *Multiracial couples.* Thousand Oaks, CA: Sage.
Describes the experiences of interracial couples, including opposition from both African American and European American family members, racism in the workplace, and institutional racism.

FAMILY STRENGTHS

University of Nebraska-Lincoln. University of Nebraska-Lincoln for Families. UNLforFamilies.unl.edu
Based on research focusing on thousands of strong families in the United States and around the world, this Web site outlines the major qualities of strong families: appreciation and affection; positive communication; commitment to the family; enjoyable time together; a sense of spiritual well-being; and the ability to manage stress and crisis effectively. Activities and resources are then presented to develop each of these important couple and family strengths.

FAMILY STRESS

Boss, P. (2002). *Family stress management: A contextual approach.* Thousand Oaks, CA: Sage.
Why do some families survive stressful situations while others fall apart?

MARRIAGE AND FAMILY THERAPY, AND EDUCATION

American Association for Marriage and Family Therapy. http://www. aamft.org
AAMFT is the key national organization for advancing the professional interests of marriage and family therapists, and has excellent educational resources for professionals and laypersons on its Web site. Washington, DC.

Olson, D. H., & Olson, A. K. (2000). *Empowering couples: Building on your strengths.* Minneapolis: Life Innovations.

PARENTHOOD

Deutsch, F. M. (1999). *Halving it all: How equally shared parenting works.* Cambridge, MA: Harvard University Press.
Focuses on what helps couples maintain equal responsibilities and involvement with children and equal time to pursue work outside the home.

Dinkmeyer, D. C., & MacKay, G. D. (1996). *Raising a responsible child: How to prepare your child for today's complex world.* New York: Simon & Schuster.
Revised edition of a very popular book for parents.

Faber, A. (1998). *Siblings without rivalry: How to help your children live together so you can live too.* New York: Avon Books.

Frank, R. (1999). *The involved father: Family-tested solutions for getting dads to participate more in the daily lives of their children.* New York: St. Martin's Press.
A delightful book on how to achieve balanced parenting.

Peters, H. E., & Day, R. D. (Eds.). (2000). *Fatherhood: Research, interventions, and policies*. New York: The Haworth Press.
Articles in the volume examine the many faces of fatherhood.

RELATIONSHIPS

Ciaramigoi, A. P., & Ketcham, K. (2000). *The power of empathy: A practical guide for creating intimacy, self-understanding, and lasting love in your life*. New York: Dutton.
This book summarizes why and how empathy can lead to more healthy love relationships.

Gottman, J. M., & DeClaire, J. (2001). *The relationship cure: A five-step guide for building better connections with family, friends, and lovers*. New York: Crown.

Lerner, H. (2001). *The dance of connection*. New York: HarperCollins.
This book offers practical suggestions for how to talk to someone when you are mad, hurt, frustrated, or scared.

Markman, H. H., Stanley, S., & Blumberg, S. L. (2001). *Fighting for your marriage*. San Francisco: Jossey-Bass.
Provides an overview of the authors' PREP communication program for couples; contains very useful suggestions for resolving couple conflict.

McManus, M. J. (1995). *Marriage savers: Helping your friends and family avoid divorce*. Grand Rapids, MI: Zondervan.

Olson, D. H., & DeFrain, J. (2006). *Marriages and families: Intimacy, diversity, and strengths* (5th ed.). New York: McGraw-Hill.
A comprehensive text on marriage and family relationships from a strengths-based perspective.

SEXUAL ABUSE

Courtois, C. (1999). *Recollections of sexual abuse: Treatment, principles and guidelines*. New York: Norton.

Koenig, L. J., Doll, L. S., O'Leary, A., & Pequegnat, W. (2004). *From child sexual abuse to adult sexual risk: Trauma, revictimization, and intervention.* Washington, DC: American Psychological Association.
The relation between child sexual abuse and adult sexual health outcomes in men and women.

National Center for PTSD. Child sexual abuse. www.ncptsd.va.gov/facts/specific/fs_child_sexual_abuse.html

TRAUMA AND RESILIENCE

Bonanno, G. A. (2004). Loss, trauma, and human resilience: Have we underestimated the human capacity to thrive after extremely aversive events? *American Psychologist, 59*(1), 20-28.
Many people are exposed to loss or potentially traumatic events at some point in their lives, and yet they continue to have positive emotional experiences in life and show only minor disruptions in their ability to function.

DeFrain, J., Jones, J. E., Skogrand, L., & DeFrain, N. (2003). Surviving and transcending a traumatic childhood: An exploratory study. *Marriage and Family Review, 35*(1/2), 117-146.

McCubbin, H. I., Thompson, E. A., Thompson, A. I., & Futrell, J. A. (Eds.). (1999). *The dynamics of resilient families.* Thousand Oaks, CA: Sage.

Walsh, F. (1998). *Strengthening family resilience.* New York: Guilford Press.

Appendix B

A Self-Study Guide

It is clear from reading the stories of the people who participated in this study that the process of surviving and transcending a traumatic childhood is long and, generally, very painful. Many who have transcended and become healthy adults told us the process can also be rewarding. It can help to develop a person's sense of empathy and it can help in understanding the pain of others.

Most participants told us that writing about their experiences was helpful in that they could reflect on where they had been, where they were currently, and where they were going in the future. When we are in the middle of change, growth, or healing, we may not take the time for reflection. Some people told us that as they completed their written testimony, they identified things that still caused them pain, and they talked with a trusted friend or therapist who helped them in the healing process. As one man who participated in the study said, it may "shed light into all the dark places."

This study guide includes many of the questions that were in the questionnaire completed by the participants in the study. This tool may be helpful to anyone who experienced trauma in childhood. It may also be helpful to anyone who has experienced a painful time at any point in their life and is in the process of healing.

If you choose to complete the study guide, begin by finding a place and time that is comfortable and where you will not be interrupted. Know that this process may take you to places you have not been and places that are not fun to visit. Expect that it might cause pain—and also growth. Take several sheets of paper and just start writing the answers. Do not worry about grammar or spelling, and do not worry about whether things are in the right order. This story is about you and for you, not someone else. Stop if necessary and get back to it later. Or, at some point in the process you may choose to throw what you have written in the waste basket and not complete it at all.

Surviving and Transcending a Traumatic Childhood
© 2007 by The Haworth Press, Inc. All rights reserved.
doi:10.1300/5839_11

Keep in mind that talking to a person whom you trust might help when you get stuck, when you get angry, when the pain is too great, or when you want to celebrate new understandings and accomplishments. We also encourage you to keep a copy of your story. You might want to revisit it in a few months or several years and see where you have come in your journey towards healing. Sometime we do not realize our progress until we have some point of reference some time in the past.

1. Describe the trauma or difficult times you experienced. What exactly happened? How did you feel about yourself? How did you feel about others who were involved in the experiences?
2. How have you gotten to where you are today? What did you do personally to get through it? What did others do to help you?
3. In summary, list the key things that have made a difference in your progress of becoming a healthy adult.
4. Did you view the event or events as traumatic when they were occurring?
5. Did other people know what you were going through? How did they respond?
6. Were there people who made it more difficult for you? What specifically did they do?
7. Were there people who were helpful? What did they do?
8. What do you wish could have been done to make things better?
9. If you needed to talk to someone, who did you turn to?
10. Were there groups or activities that helped you get through this difficult time in your life?
11. What were the personal strengths or ways of looking at the world which helped you through this time?
12. How have your childhood experiences influenced any religious or spiritual beliefs you may have?
13. What role, if any, did therapists or support groups have in your process of surviving and transcending?
14. Have you ever felt personal guilt regarding what happened to you?
15. Have you ever created chaos in your life or the lives of others to create a distraction away from the emotional pain of the trauma?
16. Do you have the ability to develop close relationships with other people today? Was this affected by what happened to you?
17. Have your childhood experiences affected your decision to be involved in a committed relationship or to marry? Please explain.
18. Have your childhood experiences affected your thoughts about being a parent or your actions as a parent? Please explain.
19. How have your childhood experiences affected your relationships with other members of your nuclear and/or extended family?

20. Have your difficult childhood experiences affected your sexual life in any way? Please explain.
21. Please explain if, or how, these experiences have influenced your job or career choices in life.
22. Do you have fears or phobias as a result of what happened to you?
23. Do you have physical health problems that you believe are related to your childhood experiences?
24. Do you have so-called flashbacks about what happened to you? How often do they occur? What people or events tend to trigger these memories?
25. Do you have nightmares related to your childhood trauma? If so, what happens to you in these nightmares?
26. Do you ever have positive dreams about your situation?
27. Describe your comfort level regarding talking about your childhood with others?
28. All things considered, do you see your childhood trauma as positively or negatively affecting your life? Please explain.
29. Please write a story which best illustrates how your childhood experiences affected your life overall. Take all the time and space you need. Tell it any way that is comfortable for you.
30. What can you say about forgiveness now?
31. Have you resolved all of the issues you have had to deal with related to your traumatic childhood? What issues still exist?
32. Are you different from other people because of your experiences? If so, what is different?
33. Which of the following qualities describe you today?
    a. I have confidence in my ability to deal with most problems in my life.
    b. I have the strength to make my way through emotionally painful experiences in life.
    c. I have the capacity to see opportunities for growth, even in situations where there is pain and suffering.
    d. I have the ability to interact positively with other people.
    e. I believe other people like me.
    f. I am able to maintain a positive vision of a meaningful life.
    g. I feel good about the work I do in life.
    h. I have a high level of self-esteem.
34. Are you doing okay today? How do you know?
35. All things considered, have you survived, or have you survived *and* transcended a traumatic childhood? Please explain.
36. What still hurts today? When does it hurt? Why? What are you doing to alleviate your pain? Who might be able to help you?
37. What good things have you learned about life?
38. What good things have you learned about yourself?

39. What advice would you give to someone else who has experienced a traumatic childhood?
40. What do you think the future will bring?

We know that answering these probing questions about a very painful time in your life has been difficult. We hope the experience has been helpful and has shed light on the progress you have already made in transcending. It may also have helped you identify some lingering issues that are yet to be resolved—for it seems the healing process is never completely done.

References

Browne, A., & Finkelhor, D. (1986). Impact of child sexual abuse: A review of the research, *Psychological Bulletin, 99,* 66-67.

Darkness to Light (2006). What is child sexual abuse? Retrieved November 21, 2006 from www.d2l.org/KnowAbout/child-sexual-abuse.asp

Faulkner, W. (1965). Nobel prize speech, December 10, 1950. In J. B. Meriwether, (Ed.), *Essays, speeches, and public letters.* New York: Random House.

Gelles, R. J. (2000). Family violence. In M. H. Tonry (Ed.), *The handbook of crime and punishment* (pp. 178-206). New York: Oxford University Press.

Hemingway, E. (1929). *A farewell to arms.* New York: Charles Scribner's Sons.

James, J., & James, M. (1992). *Passions of life: Psychology and the human spirit.* New York: Plume Publishing.

Kennedy, P., & C. Crebing. (2002). Abuse and religious experience: A study of religiously committed evangelical adults. *Mental Health, Religion, and Culture* 5(3): 225-237.

Oz, S. (2001). When the wife was sexually abused as a child: Marital relations before and during her therapy for abuse. *Sexual and Relationship Therapy,* 16(3): 287-298.

Skogrand, L., Singh, A., Allgood, S., DeFrain, J., DeFrain, N., & Jones. (2005). *The process of transcending a traumatic childhood.* Unpublished manuscript.

Valentine, L., & Feinauer, L. (1993). Resilience factors associated with female survivors of childhood sexual abuse. *American Journal of Family Therapy, 21,* 216-224.

Wampler, K. S., & Nelson, B. S. (2000). *The relation of unresolved loss and childhood abuse to current relationship functioning in clinic couples.* Conference paper presented at the 62nd Annual Conference of the National Council on Family Relations, Minneapolis, MN: Nov. 8-13.

Surviving and Transcending a Traumatic Childhood
© 2007 by The Haworth Press, Inc. All rights reserved.
doi:10.1300/5839_12

Index

Dear Customer:

Please fill out & return this form to receive special deals & publishing opportunities for you! These include:
- availability of new books in your local bookstore or online
- one-time prepublication discounts
- free or heavily discounted related titles
- free samples of related Haworth Press periodicals
- publishing opportunities in our periodicals or Book Division

❑ OK! Please keep me on your regular mailing list and/or e-mailing list for new announcements!

Name _____

Address_____

STAPLE OR TAPE YOUR BUSINESS CARD HERE!

_____

*E-mail address _____
*Your e-mail address will never be rented, shared, exchanged, sold, or divested. You may "opt-out" at any time.
May we use your e-mail address for confirmations and other types of information? ❑ Yes ❑ No

Special needs:
Describe below any special information you would like:
- Forthcoming professional/textbooks
- New popular books
- Publishing opportunities in academic periodicals
- Free samples of periodicals in my area(s)

Special needs/Special areas of interest:

_____

_____

_____

_____

Please contact me as soon as possible. I have a special requirement/project:

_____

_____

_____

_____

The Haworth Press, Inc.

) PLEASE COMPLETE THE FORM ABOVE AND MAIL TO:
Donna Barnes, Marketing Dept., The Haworth Press, Inc.
10 Alice Street, Binghamton, NY 13904–1580 USA
Tel: 1–800–429–6784 • Outside US/Canada Tel: (607) 722–5857
Fax: 1–800–895–0582 • Outside US/Canada Fax: (607) 771–0012
E-mail: orders@HaworthPress.com

GBIC07